## Praise for *Make Your School Irresistible*

"This wise, grounded, clear, and organized book is both an invitation to action and a plan for school leaders who want to work with faculty to create and live out a worthy story about what their school stands for—to demonstrate why their story matters to everyone in the community served by the school. The book provides a trustworthy compass for envisioning, enacting, tending, and nurturing the story over time. *Make Your School Irresistible* made me wonder why all school leaders don't do all these things all the time, even as it led me to understand that many of us have needed this guide all along."

—**Carol Ann Tomlinson,** William Clay Parrish Jr. Professor Emeritus, School of Education and Human Development, University of Virginia; and co-author, *Leading for Differentiation: Growing Teachers Who Grow Kids*

"*Make Your School Irresistible* provides education leaders with a rationale, tools, and strategies that can be put into practice immediately to address the critical educator labor market issue schools are facing today. The authors recognize that it is now an educator's market, and it is time to shift the focus to inviting, investing, and inspiring so that schools are magnets for the highest-quality educators who can make the greatest impact on student learning. This is a great advocacy tool and resource for any school leader, school leadership team, or district leader who supports school leaders and coaches."

—**Dr. Sharon Roberts,** president, Leadership Innovations Inc.; senior advisor, SCORE

"In *Make Your School Irresistible*, the authors offer a dynamic, practical approach to transforming school culture. As an instructional coach at a hard-to-staff Title I middle school, I've seen firsthand how their strategies invite, invest, and inspire educators to thrive. This book is an invaluable resource for leaders committed to building a supportive, engaging school environment."

—**Dr. Jasmine Everett,** instructional coach at a Title I middle school

"In a world swirling with opinions about education, there's something we can agree on: We need great teachers. But how can we find and keep teachers when district budgets are tight and time is scarce? Here's the good news: There *are* things we can do! Carrie and Jessica have curated a sizable collection of practical strategies that stand the test of time. Oh, the good that this book will do!"

—**Tanny McGregor,** educator and author, *Ink and Ideas: Sketchnotes for Engagement, Comprehension, and Thinking*

"In this cutting-edge text, Carrie Bishop and Jessica Holloway emphasize that retaining teachers means inspiring them to grow as leaders and nurturing their potential, even if it means letting them soar and move on to new opportunities. By supporting highly effective teachers in pursuing their own goals, leaders not only retain talent in the short term but also contribute to a culture of growth and lifelong learning that strengthens the entire educational community."

—**William D. Kennedy,** former vice president for Leadership Initiatives and director, Principal Leadership Academy, Public Education Foundation; former teacher, assistant principal, and principal, Hamilton County (TN) Schools

"In a time when teacher retention is more critical than ever, this guide is a beacon of hope for creating schools where everyone feels seen, supported, and valued. Educational leaders looking to inspire and sustain long-term success will find this book to be an invaluable resource."

—**Kelly Hastings,** implementation leadership coach

"*Make Your School Irresistible* is a must-have for school administrators focused on teacher retention. It provides practical tools for building a strong, empowered faculty culture; clear assessments; and action steps for real impact. Having collaborated with Jessica, I've seen how effective these strategies can be, especially in my school's journey toward STEM Designation through the Tennessee Department of Education. This book offers invaluable guidance for any leader committed to retaining excellent teachers and driving positive change."

—**Jeremy Jones,** principal, Valley View Elementary School, Cleveland, TN

# Make Your School
# Irresistible

# Make Your School Irresistible

## The Secret to Attracting and Retaining Great Teachers

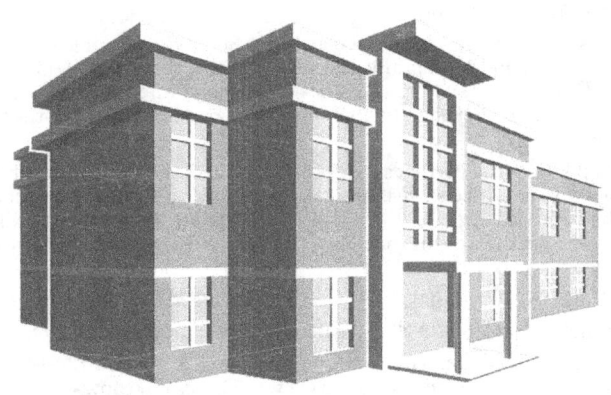

Carrie Bishop and
Jessica Holloway

Arlington, Virginia USA

2800 Shirlington Road, Suite 1001 • Arlington, VA 22206 USA
Phone: 800-933-2723 or 703-578-9600 • Fax: 703-575-5400
Website: www.ascd.org • Email: member@ascd.org
Author guidelines: www.ascd.org/write

Richard Culatta, *Chief Executive Officer;* Anthony Rebora, *Chief Content Officer;* Genny Ostertag, *Managing Director, Book Acquisitions & Editing;* Susan Hills, *Senior Acquisitions Editor;* Mary Beth Nielsen, *Director, Book Editing;* Jennifer L. Morgan, *Editor;* Catherine Gillespie, *Graphic Designer;* Valerie Younkin, *Senior Production Designer;* Kelly Marshall, *Production Manager;* Shajuan Martin, *E-Publishing Specialist;* Kathryn Oliver, *Creative Project Manager*

Copyright © 2025 ASCD. All rights reserved. It is illegal to reproduce copies of this work in print or electronic format (including reproductions displayed on a secure intranet or stored in a retrieval system or other electronic storage device from which copies can be made or displayed) without the prior written permission of the publisher. By purchasing only authorized electronic or print editions and not participating in or encouraging piracy of copyrighted materials, you support the rights of authors and publishers. Readers who wish to reproduce or republish excerpts of this work in print or electronic format may do so for a small fee by contacting the Copyright Clearance Center (CCC), 222 Rosewood Dr., Danvers, MA 01923, USA (phone: 978-750-8400; fax: 978-646-8600; web: www.copyright.com). To inquire about site licensing options or any other reuse, contact ASCD Permissions at www.ascd.org/permissions or permissions@ascd.org. For a list of vendors authorized to license ASCD ebooks to institutions, see www.ascd.org/epubs. Send translation inquiries to translations@ascd.org.

ASCD® is a registered trademark of Association for Supervision and Curriculum Development. All other trademarks contained in this book are the property of, and reserved by, their respective owners, and are used for editorial and informational purposes only. No such use should be construed to imply sponsorship or endorsement of the book by the respective owners.

All web links in this book are correct as of the publication date below but may have become inactive or otherwise modified since that time. If you notice a deactivated or changed link, please email books@ascd.org with the words "Link Update" in the subject line. In your message, please specify the web link, the book title, and the page number on which the link appears.

PAPERBACK ISBN: 978-1-4166-3352-5    ASCD product #124012 n1/25

PDF EBOOK ISBN: 978-1-4166-3353-2; see Books in Print for other formats.

Quantity discounts are available: email programteam@ascd.org or call 800-933-2723, ext. 5773, or 703-575-5773. For desk copies, go to www.ascd.org/deskcopy.

**Library of Congress Cataloging-in-Publication Data**
Names: Bishop, Carrie (Instructional coach), author. | Holloway, Jessica, author.
Title: Make your school irresistible : the secret to attracting and retaining great teachers / Carrie Bishop and Jessica Holloway.
Description: Arlington, Virginia, USA : ASCD, [2025] | Includes bibliographical references and index.
Identifiers: LCCN 2024047602 (print) | LCCN 2024047603 (ebook) | ISBN 9781416633525 (paperback) | ISBN 9781416633532 (pdf)
Subjects: LCSH: Teacher turnover. | Teachers—Selection and improvement.
Classification: LCC LB2833 .B78 2025 (print) | LCC LB2833 (ebook) | DDC 371.14—dc23/eng/20241210
LC record available at https://lccn.loc.gov/2024047602
LC ebook record available at https://lccn.loc.gov/2024047603

34  33  32  31  30  29  28  27  26  25          1  2  3  4  5  6  7  8  9  10  11  12

# Make Your School Irresistible

The Secret to Attracting and Retaining Great Teachers

Introduction: Invite, Invest, Inspire . . . . . . . . . . . . . . . . . . . . . . . . . . . . 1

1. Unveiling Identity . . . . . . . . . . . . . . . . . . . . . . . . . . . . . . . . . . . . . . . 7

2. Inviting Excellence . . . . . . . . . . . . . . . . . . . . . . . . . . . . . . . . . . . . . 23

3. Welcoming New Team Members . . . . . . . . . . . . . . . . . . . . . . . . . 48

4. Prioritizing People . . . . . . . . . . . . . . . . . . . . . . . . . . . . . . . . . . . . . 76

5. Believing in Your Team . . . . . . . . . . . . . . . . . . . . . . . . . . . . . . . . 102

6. Igniting an Eternal Flame . . . . . . . . . . . . . . . . . . . . . . . . . . . . . . 126

7. Building Capacity . . . . . . . . . . . . . . . . . . . . . . . . . . . . . . . . . . . . . 148

Conclusion: Your Next Steps in Inviting,
Investing, and Inspiring . . . . . . . . . . . . . . . . . . . . . . . . . . . . . . . . . . 165

Appendix: Sample Peer Observation Tools . . . . . . . . . . . . . . . . . . . 167

References . . . . . . . . . . . . . . . . . . . . . . . . . . . . . . . . . . . . . . . . . . . . . 170

Index . . . . . . . . . . . . . . . . . . . . . . . . . . . . . . . . . . . . . . . . . . . . . . . . . . 172

About the Authors . . . . . . . . . . . . . . . . . . . . . . . . . . . . . . . . . . . . . . . 177

# Introduction:
# Invite, Invest, Inspire

Highly effective teachers are essential to student success. As many teachers leave the profession, either for other careers (in what has become known as the Great Resignation) or by retiring, schools must reimagine their standard procedures for filling vacant faculty positions. It's no longer sufficient to recruit teachers and expect to be done with the work. Implementing retention practices is critical because replacing teachers lost through turnover is much harder. It's time to reframe faculty hiring practices to communicate to teacher candidates the benefits a position holds for them, rather than solely focusing on what they can bring to you.

With such a seismic shift taking place in schools across the country, educators have options. How, then, can you make your school the most attractive choice to job seekers? We offer three words: *invite, invest,* and *inspire*. Throughout this book, these three concepts form a framework that you can use to increase the potential for you and your school to build a faculty that is knowledgeable, empowered, and stable.

Chapters 1 and 2 focus on shifting your methods of inviting educators to work at your school from the standard recruitment practices that focus solely on how great the school is to ones that demonstrate how great the school is *for the candidate*. Chapters 3, 4, and 5 explore the value of investing in educators and moving from a mindset that believes everyone is replaceable to one that focuses on prioritizing individual needs and creating a culture that promotes belonging and esteem. Chapters 6 and 7 address the advantages of inspiring educators by offering personalized support and growth, which can simultaneously move them forward in their career.

## The Current Educational Landscape

Recent reports on teacher recruitment and retention in the United States are not promising. Between the 2021–22 and 2022–23 school years, eight states experienced the highest rate of departure from the education profession in at least five years (Barnum, 2023). This exodus was accompanied by a significant number of teachers seriously contemplating quitting. The first annual Merrimack College Teacher Survey, taken in January and February 2022, was a comprehensive national poll involving more than 1,300 teachers. Commissioned by the School of Education and Social Policy at Merrimack College, it was conducted by the nonprofit, nonpartisan EdWeek Research Center. In her analysis of the survey, Kurtz (2022) highlights a startling statistic: "Forty-four percent of teachers say they are very or fairly likely to leave the profession in the next two years, up from 29 percent in the 2011 MetLife survey" (para. 12). This finding pushes us to reconsider what needs to be done to keep teachers in the profession.

In the National Center for Education Statistics *Report on the Condition of Education 2023*, Irwin and colleagues (2023) state that from 2012–13 to 2019–20, there was a notable 28 percent decrease in the number of individuals completing traditional teacher preparation programs, and schools experienced increasing difficulty in filling open positions. These findings highlight a concerning downward trend in the availability of certified educators and a declining interest in education as a profession.

This imbalance between supply and demand can lead to various consequences, including increased competition for scarce resources. In the economic sphere, scarcity is a fundamental concept that influences decision making. When a resource becomes scarce, its perceived value tends to rise, leading to changes in pricing, allocation, and prioritization. Fewer teachers to hire means fiercer competition among schools and districts. Scarcity can also drive innovation and a search for alternative solutions to meet the demand for limited resources.

In response to this scarcity of educators, we urge you to consider what your school can do to attract and retain educators who will contribute to your mission and vision—and how you will reciprocate by furthering theirs. Our goal is to help you make your school irresistible by creating a community that educators want to be a part of and one that nurtures their best selves.

## Valuing Educators' Voices

The overarching goal of this book is to offer guidance on fostering a professional environment where educators find fulfillment and feel genuinely valued so that they will do their best for their students. We believe in elevating educators' voices and seek to recognize and amplify the perspectives, experiences, and insights of both teachers and school leaders. Teachers and staff often share with coaches the feedback that school leaders need to hear. In our capacity as school-based and district-level coaches, we came to realize the benefits that could be reaped by categorizing this feedback and distilling it into actionable steps. To further our collection of useful guidance, we surveyed current and retired educators at all levels, from the classroom to the district office, in both public and private schools, as well as consultants and business owners. Our results form the core of this book.

In addition to valuing their voices, we want educators to be fulfilled. Some educators transition out of teaching because of a lack of opportunities for change or challenge. Others are leaving particular schools or abandoning the profession altogether due to factors that can be addressed without spending more money or requiring special programs. We chose to focus on strategies to invite, invest, and inspire that are *within school leaders' realm of control and influence.* These practical and actionable insights are designed to empower leaders at the school level to create a supportive environment for their educators. We firmly believe that implementing these strategies can contribute to retaining talented people and cultivating a culture of continuous improvement and professional growth within the broader educational community. Ultimately, our intent is to provide leaders with tools that will enhance teacher satisfaction, foster a positive school culture, and elevate the overall educational experience for students and faculty.

## Acting Within Our Scope

The strategies we present here are constricted to the realms that are within school leaders' immediate control and influence. Although factors such as compensation structures, legislative decisions, and overarching education policies undoubtedly play crucial roles in schools' particular contexts, our focus will remain on practical strategies and approaches that most school leaders can implement directly. This targeted approach ensures that school leaders can actively engage with and apply the concepts we present, creating a hands-on, applicable, and useful resource.

## How to Use This Book

As a practical resource for creating a supportive and empowering environment for educators, this book is organized to allow you to navigate chapters based on their relevance to your current situation. Each chapter addresses specific challenges. If a particular challenge or area of improvement applies to your school's situation, you can delve directly into the corresponding chapters and try one or two new strategies at a time. Remember that to successfully integrate these strategies into your school culture will require gradual, consistent practice.

### Real-Life Insights

Each chapter also features quotes from practicing educators in various professional roles to help establish its tone or context. Listening to educators' contributions to the ongoing dialogue about best practices, challenges, and solutions in education is essential. The relatable insights and perspectives shared in this book are grounded in real-world challenges and may shed some light on issues you are facing. They also reinforce the idea of effective leadership having a positive impact in a variety of ways.

## Self-Assessment

As you begin reading each chapter, we recommend that you evaluate your current practices in a particular aspect of recruitment and retention with a brief self-assessment. The response scale ranges from 1 (strongly disagree) to 5 (strongly agree). We encourage you to engage in honest reflection and use your discoveries to improve your current practices or implement new ones.

## Actions to Implement

Throughout the chapters, we've included Try This sections with strategies or activities to implement. We have used these practices in our own coaching work, co-created them with other educators, or witnessed their use by effective leaders. The strategies require either no or minimal funds. Before you jump into taking action, however, we encourage you to focus on quality over quantity. Instead of pursuing a myriad of changes simultaneously, increase the likelihood of successful implementation by focusing on high-priority activities that align with your school's mission and vision. Once you identify an area for growth, select a strategy or an activity to implement, reflect on, and refine.

## Walking in Someone Else's Shoes

You will also encounter Empathy Episodes, problematic scenarios that offer a valuable opportunity to develop empathy, an essential aspect of effective leadership. Each scenario is accompanied by reflection questions designed to prompt thoughtful consideration of the emotional and professional impact of the stories and to give you a deeper understanding of your team's experiences.

As you read through the Empathy Episodes, immerse yourself in the emotions and challenges portrayed. Approach the vignettes as an opportunity to step into team members' shoes and gain insight into their perspectives. Take a moment to think about the varying viewpoints of the individuals in the scenario and apply what you've learned from the chapter content to consider how an effective leader could have created a positive environment for the educator involved.

As your leadership evolves, the ability to empathize with your team's experiences will remain a crucial aspect of fostering a positive and inclusive school culture.

## Commitment

Toward the end of each chapter, we ask the following questions about your commitment to the practices discussed:

- What strategies from this chapter are you committed to implementing?
- Who can help you implement these strategies?
- What outcome do you want to see as a result of implementing these strategies?

Use these questions to pause, capture your thinking, and plan actions for implementation.

## Summary

Each chapter ends with a summary that highlights key ideas and connects to the subsequent chapter. These summaries can also serve as a preview or review for those who read the book out of order or over an extended period of time.

Happy reading and leading!

# 1

# Unveiling Identity

*My instructional focus is on immigrant-origin students and multilanguage learners. I was drawn to work in schools because of the large enrollment of multilanguage learners. The community identity centered on families experiencing poverty and enrolled a majority of students of color.*

—Donna Neary, teacher of English as a New Language

The district we work in reported 549 job openings in February 2023. Although some were immediate openings and some were for the following year, a need for 549 new hires is notable. The 76 schools in our district compete to attract and retain high-quality educators who will transform the lives of almost 45,000 students and their families. Because today's students are tomorrow's workforce, the value of a well-trained, effective teacher is higher now than ever. Today's education graduates entertain multiple job offers and choices about where to work, as do veteran educators and top talent seeking to relocate.

A strong school identity communicates to potential applicants what the school values. What makes your school different from others? What first impression do outsiders take from your school? Schools that broadcast their vision are more likely to attract desirable candidates who share the school's values and want to help move its mission forward.

This chapter focuses on school culture and identity—how to tell your school's story, establish your brand, and communicate your purpose with others. Long before you conduct interviews with candidates, you should be sharing the story of your school with every audience you can. Be prepared to use every interaction with both potential employees and the greater community as an opportunity to network on behalf of your school. As a school leader, leverage formal and informal opportunities to talk about your school, because you never know who might be listening. And never underestimate the powers of social media and digital presence; we will explore the significant impact of these tools later in the chapter.

## What Is Your School's Identity?

School identity is more than a name or a school's most recent test scores. We want to know who the school is as an entity. What makes your school what it is?

All schools are relatively similar in operation. They're generally charged with educating children so that they're prepared to enter the workforce, trade school, military service, or college. But no two school staffs are the same, nor do schools serve identical student populations. So what is *your* school's identity? If we asked a community member about your school, what would they say?

Use the statements in Figure 1.1 to reflect on how your school is perceived in the broader community. Consider the clarity of your school's identity, the accuracy of the traits attributed to your school, and the effectiveness of your storytelling in communicating your school's purpose. Your insights can play a pivotal role in shaping a more authentic, resonant narrative for your educational institution.

We'd like to spotlight two particular schools in our community. Both demonstrate unwavering clarity in their identity. They not only boast top-notch academic achievements but also shine as examples of a well-defined and purposeful school culture. We invite you to explore the stories of these schools, where identity isn't just a concept but a living, breathing testament to their commitment to excellence.

**FIGURE 1.1**

**School Identity Self-Assessment**

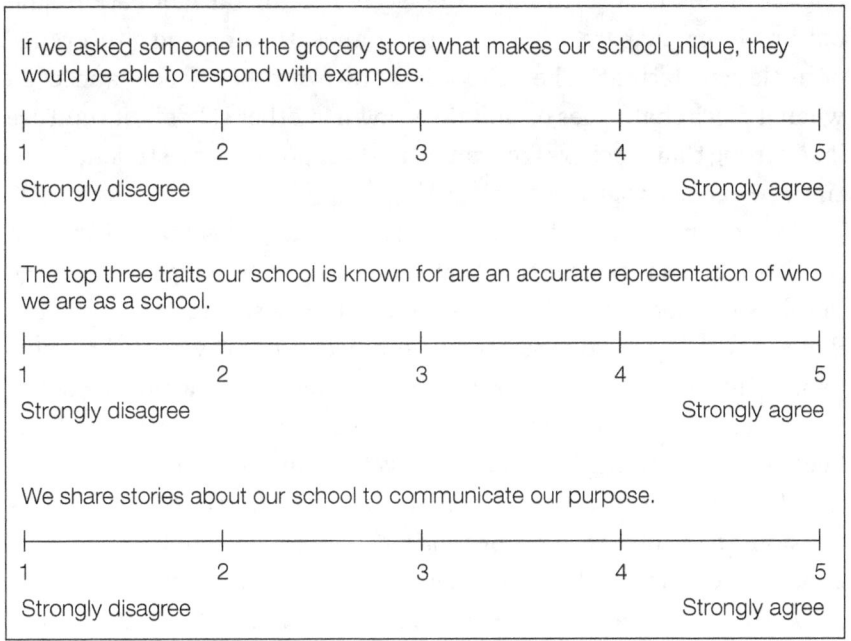

The first example is a nationally recognized public magnet school for grades 6–12. Students audition for admission in one of the following fine arts concentrations: acting, communications, dance, instrumental music, musical theater, visual arts, vocal music, and technical theater. The school has an equally rigorous academic program, with high expectations for all students. It's a beacon for the arts, and arts and academics share center stage. This school is well-known and successfully attracts top talent and scholars. Anyone in our community can tell you what this school is about.

Another school in our community with a strong identity is a K–8 magnet school whose success dramatically elevated property values and whose desirability is such that parents camp out to enter their student in the admissions lottery. The school engages students in real-world, project-based learning experiences, supported by weekly learning expeditions thanks to a partnership between the school and six area museums. The school itself becomes a museum four times a year, showcasing and celebrating student learning. Students have opportunities in foreign language, access to digital fabrication, and options to participate in music/band, dance, theater, and a full range of athletic offerings. The school is known for excellence, and even when it faces challenges or morale is down at other schools, its culture is so strong that teachers feel valued and supported, and students continue to experience the joy of learning.

Notice that both of these examples are magnet schools. Inherent in such schools is the concept that something is drawing or attracting families to choose these options instead of the school in their attendance zone. If a family moving into our community says their student is interested in the arts, we immediately know which school to recommend, as do real estate agents and other community members, because the branding is so clear and well communicated.

What attracts families to *your* school? Quick: Recite your school's mission or vision. Are you hesitating? If so, you're not alone. Most educators cannot recite their school's mission or vision statement. For most, the words have become wallpaper or text on a letterhead. Even if the mission or vision statement exists in your head, does it exist in your heart? Your heart holds the *why*; your head holds the *how*. School culture is anchored to your *why*, which may be shaped by a mission or vision statement, a list of beliefs, or a just cause. If you're uncertain of your school's purpose, others will be too.

Let's look at some powerful sentence frames that can bridge the gap between the common challenge of merely stating a school's vision to actively shaping and embodying that vision. These frames can serve as strategic tools, allowing you to zoom in on your school's purpose and transform abstract ideals into tangible guiding principles. Here are some examples:

- At *[name of school]* you can rely on us to _____.
- The community has come to expect _____ from our school.
- When students leave our school, we want future teachers/employers to say that our students are _____.
- We base our decisions on the belief that _____.
- Our promise to our students is _____.

Of course, these sentence frames are not the only path to identifying your school's purpose. However you approach it, we encourage you to spend time articulating your school's purpose and identity. *Heart* work is *hard* work, but knowing your collective *why* will strengthen who you are as a school and what you do as a school community.

It's also important to remember that people pay attention to what you do, not just to what you say. Actions and traditions often reveal and reflect a school's identity and purpose. Consider whether your school's traditions need updating or redesigning to remain aligned with the school's current purpose. Remember that annually held events communicate your school's values, and the community will come to expect those exchanges. For example, if service is integral to your school identity, examine what traditions you have established or need to establish to connect with that purpose. What types of celebrations does your school hold (e.g., arts performances, award ceremonies) to demonstrate what your community values? Lastly, does your school's schedule reflect your priorities? For example, people will find it difficult to recognize a school as having a STEM identity if classes focusing on science, technology, engineering, and math are not evident in the schedule. You may want to make your school's schedule public to further communicate your purpose. Remember, people hear what you *say* but believe in what you *do*. Be sure that what you do speaks just as loudly as what you say.

## What Is Your School's Story?

Once you're clear about your school's identity, shift to exploring your school's story. Reputation often precedes reality. You can positively influence your school's reputation by sharing stories and celebrating successes. Communicate your positives so loudly that the negatives must struggle to be heard. You may be hesitant to jump into storytelling, but it's important to remember that if you're not telling your school's story, you're letting others do it for you—and what they say may not accurately reflect your school.

Humans are biologically and neurologically wired to connect with stories, which makes well-told stories irresistible. Compare the following two television commercials. Commercial A shows a sick person in bed. The voiceover focuses on the list of symptoms a particular medication will address, and the ad ends with the person feeling better. Commercial B shows a mom lying in bed, coughing and looking around the house at everything that needs to be done. She needs to get well quickly to tackle her to-do list. She takes the medicine, naps, and awakens without a cough—smiling and ready to go. The commercial ends with her making cookies with her kids. Which commercial would linger in your mind? Which product would you be more likely to purchase?

Ultimately, you want people to be moved by your purpose, which requires developing a compelling story. In *Stories That Stick*, Kindra Hall (2019) explains four components of a great story: "identifiable characters, authentic emotion, a significant moment, and specific details" (p. 41). Regardless of the type of story being told, the audience should be able to relate to the characters and feel genuine emotion while being transported to a certain place and time in order to visualize the experience. A compelling story pulls people in and takes them on a journey as if they're experiencing it firsthand.

Use print, video, and audio formats to capture your school's story and package it for your intended audience. Testimonials and brochure-type content work well on school websites and social media. Remember that not all the stories you collect will be "front-page ready." Some may miss the mark, and you may need to gather many tales to find the right one for the right time. When you do find the right one, however, you will know by the impression it leaves on the hearts and minds of its audience.

Remember, if you're not telling your stories, someone else will, and they might not be the ones you want told. The following sections offer some suggestions for stories that will reflect your school's purpose and identity.

### Staff Success Stories

Have all staff write a success story that zooms in on specific actions that resulted in a successful outcome for students or staff. The story should answer questions such as these: What obstacle was tackled? What unique conditions at our school contributed to success in this case? What actions were taken? How did success evolve over time?

Ask staff to document key actions and dialogue with a timeline. Annotating the timeline with facial expressions can portray how those involved felt throughout the process. Ask staff to focus on how they want readers to feel after reading their story. Share these stories on social media, on your school website, in internal district communications, with local news outlets, and in school communications.

## Testimonials

Capture testimonials from families, students, community partners, and other stakeholders, including alumni, and share them on social media and the school website. Provide sentence starters such as the following to help individuals organize their contributions:

- Families
    - *[Name of school]* is a great place to learn because _____.
    - My child used to be _____ but now is _____.
    - I am confident that my child experiences _____ while at this school.
- Students
    - One of the ways *[name of school]* has affected me is _____.
    - I used to _____, but now I _____.
    - I look forward to _____ because _____.
- Community partners and other stakeholders
    - We are proud to partner with *[name of school]* because _____.
    - One of the benefits of working alongside *[name of school]* is _____.
    - When we leave *[name of school]*, we are amazed that _____.
    - As an alumnus of *[name of school]*, I am proud to see _____.

## Futurecasting Stories

A futurecasting story describes three parts of your school's story: the beginning (past), where you are now (present), and who you want to be (future). Here's an example:

*The beginning (past):* We've been a traditional school focusing on direct instruction and increasing math and literacy scores. Although we have introduced various initiatives over the past three years, we haven't seen the desired gains in student achievement.

*Where we are now (present):* We're beginning to implement STEM learning across the school. This means you might hear your student talk about the "engineering design process" or "project-based learning." As we tackle new strategies and students and staff transition to new ways of teaching and learning, we anticipate some discomfort.

*Who we want to be (future):* After working through the transition, our students will be equipped with essential skills, productive habits, and content knowledge that will better prepare them for college and careers. Our school will be known for cultivating change in our community through project-based learning.

## Leadership Stories

A leadership story can begin by sharing your professional origins, such as what inspired you to become an educator. Consider focusing on a particular person or event that sparked the joy of teaching and learning in you, and describe memorable moments and successes that affirmed your decision to be an educator. This glimpse into your passion for education will invite others to join you on your journey, humanize you, and connect you with others in your mission to have a positive impact on the school and students.

Explain *why* you're in your current position as a school leader—and be sure not to say that you are there because you were "placed" at this particular school or it was convenient for you personally. Those reasons may be true, but they should be tangential to your purpose for being a school leader—to your why. Tell your story in a way that motivates others to work alongside you. Share your vision for what the school needs to do the most good.

Finally, describe the leader you aim to be. Sharing the vision you hold for yourself will communicate both transparency and accountability. Here are some examples:

- I believe in partnering with the community to provide whole-child support.
- I am committed to equity and creating a sense of urgency to close achievement gaps.

- I want to inspire, and I welcome help in gaining buy-in to achieve our school's goals.
- I am investing in the cultural competency of our teachers and staff and in our school instruction and practices.

## What Is Your School's Brand?

What do you *see* when you hear the name "McDonald's"? You probably visualize the Golden Arches. What do you *think* when you hear the name "McDonald's"? You might think of affordable food, quick service, or Happy Meals. How would you describe the fast-food giant's reputation? You might think about broken ice cream machines, McRib sandwiches only while supplies last, or their jingle "I'm lovin' it." McDonald's has a well-established brand, and people know what to expect from the restaurants.

Now think of a school that has a really strong brand. What does this school do that communicates who they are? How do they promote or express their brand? What connection can you make between how you feel about this school and how they promote their brand?

Your school's brand is key to communicating your school's purpose, so it's important to ensure that the brand reflects that purpose. Components of a brand may include a logo, a mascot, a motto, and a mission or vision statement.

An identifiable school logo is crucial for increasing visibility. If your school does not have a logo, you can create one using digital tools such as Canva or Adobe Creative Cloud, or you can ask staff and students to submit ideas for the design. If your school already has a logo, consider whether redesigning it with new colors, shapes, and words would be worthwhile.

How can you leverage your school's mascot to share the school's purpose? The mascot can provide a theme to connect the brand and purpose. For example, if your mascot is a lion, you might use ROAR as an acronym for your core beliefs: *R*eaching goals, *O*vercoming obstacles, *A*chieving excellence, and *R*allying together. You might then share stories in a newsletter titled *Hear Us ROAR*.

A motto is another concise way to communicate your school's brand. If your motto is longer than one sentence, however, you're moving into mission statement and vision territory. Stick to something simple and clear. For example, a school known for empowering students to enact change in their local community might adopt "Creating Agents of Change" as its motto. Branding is all about what people see and hear related to the school. Make it easy for others to remember you.

Now that you've determined your school's identity, purpose, stories, and brand, it's time to think about how to share them with others. Let's look at what it takes to promote your school's brand from recognizable to memorable.

> **Try This: AI-Assisted Branding**
>
> Use an artificial intelligence (AI) tool like Google Gemini to generate ideas for branding components such as logo, motto, and mascot. You might start with a prompt like this: "Create a logo for *[school name]* that focuses on *[school focus area or motto]* using shades of *[colors]*."
>
> Once you get a response, refine the results by adding new elements or revising the initial prompt. AI tools can serve as a thought partner and provide a starting point for creating a brand that represents the school and communicates the school's purpose.

## Merchandise

Apparel, stickers, and branded items can increase your school's visibility. People wearing items featuring the school logo convey the message that they're proud to be associated with the school as a student, athlete, parent, or staff member. Stickers and magnets also show school pride. Items such as pencils and notepads branded with the school's logo and motto can serve to communicate these identifying traits to guests or prospective staff.

Along with a distinctive logo, merchandise should feature a consistent color scheme. These visual elements can be reproduced in various school materials, signage, and online platforms, as well as on merchandise, symbolizing a sense of unity and pride that students, staff, and the community can rally around.

## Digital Presence on Social Media

The rise of social media makes the need for a digital presence imperative. The goal is to meet people where they are, and that means on social media platforms such as Facebook, Instagram, and X (formerly Twitter). Telling your school's story through social media can be a powerful way to engage with your community, showcase achievements, and highlight the unique aspects of your institution. But effective use of social media doesn't happen without conscious effort. Here's how you can effectively use social media to tell your school's story.

***Develop a content strategy that aligns with your school's mission, values, and goals.***

Determine the key messages you want to convey and the audience you want to reach. Highlight student accomplishments, awards, and projects. Share photos, videos, and testimonials to celebrate success and inspire others. Introduce faculty and staff members on social media and showcase their expertise and dedication to humanize your school. Post "behind-the-scenes" content to give your followers a glimpse into daily life at your school. Share photos and videos of classroom and extracurricular activities, events, and campus facilities.

***Use storytelling to convey the unique experiences and perspectives of students, teachers, alumni, and parents.***

Share anecdotes, testimonials, and personal narratives that illustrate the impact of your school on the larger community.

***Foster meaningful connections with parents and alumni on social media by sharing updates, news, and events relevant to their interests.***

Encourage former school community members to share their own experiences and memories of your school. Promote school events, fundraisers, performances, and initiatives. Create event pages, provide reminders, and post live updates to generate excitement and attendance. Encourage students, parents, and alumni to share their own photos, stories, and experiences related to the school. Create hashtags and campaigns to facilitate user-generated content and engagement.

### Follow recommended guidelines for using social media.

Guidelines for social media include the following:

- *Be professional.* Maintain a professional demeanor on social media platforms. Remember that your posts and interactions reflect not only on you as a school leader but also on your school in general and the education profession as a whole.
- *Respect privacy.* Attend to issues of privacy for your students and colleagues. Avoid sharing sensitive or confidential information about students or discussing specific individuals without their consent.
- *Set boundaries.* Establish clear boundaries between your personal and professional social media postings by creating separate accounts for each.
- *Model digital citizenship.* Demonstrate positive digital citizenship by promoting responsible and ethical behavior online. Teach students how to use social media responsibly and safely by modeling appropriate use.
- *Follow school, district, and state policies.* Familiarize yourself with social media policies and guidelines at all levels. Ensure that your social media activities align with these policies and seek clarification if needed.
- *Monitor privacy settings.* Regularly review and update your privacy settings on social media platforms to control who can see your posts and interact with you. Doing so helps protect your personal and professional reputation.
- *Respond to feedback and inquiries.* Monitor social media channels for comments, questions, and feedback from your community. Respond promptly and courteously to address concerns, provide information, and foster positive interactions.
- *Be consistent.* Maintain a consistent posting schedule to keep your audience engaged and informed. A mix of content types and formats will keep your feed diverse and engaging.

- *Track and analyze performance.* Use the analytics features in social media platforms to track the reach of your posts and campaigns. Monitor key metrics such as engagement and demographics to understand what content resonates best with your audience and adjust your strategy accordingly.

Implementing these strategies will help you effectively use social media to tell your school's story, strengthen community connections, and showcase the positive impact of your school.

**Remember that social media needs to be tended to like a garden.**

A presence on social media requires regular and consistent maintenance. Set a day or time to post content each week. Drafting content ahead of time can expedite posting during or after events. Monitor notifications and comments to ensure timely responses or address any concerns. Enlist multiple caretakers to keep the weeds away and promote more activity and growth. Consider creating a social media team of staff members to help post the school's stories. Invite students in marketing class, yearbook club, or student government to support social media posting under the guidance and supervision of school staff.

## School Website

The school website, usually the first place people go to learn more about a school, should include the logo or mascot as a visual identifier. It's important to ensure that the website content remains timely, accurate, and attractive. Identify who will update and maintain the site and what the expectations are for upkeep. Create a schedule for regular updates and maintenance, including the removal of outdated material. Dedicate time during leadership team meetings to gather suggestions for updating website content. If the school has a webmaster, develop a structure for communicating with that person. Create a section to announce faculty and staff openings or to outline the procedure to follow for prospective employees who would like to be notified about future opportunities. Include a concise but informative and appealing description of the school for prospective employees and families to communicate the school's identity and purpose. Be sure the website includes any noteworthy designations, recognitions, awards, or other unique components. Embed links to social media posts or accounts on the website to reach a broader audience with these tools.

### Community Members

School leaders and staff should be visible in the community as school representatives. Publicize your availability to share your school's stories by speaking at local events, at meetings of civic clubs, and to local government officials. Conversely, invite community members to visit the school and share their own stories. Have a school representative attend regular meetings of community organizations. For example, attend the local chamber of commerce quarterly meetings to take advantage of the opportunity to share the school's mission, needs, and successes. Every school event is an opportunity to put your best foot forward, and attendees just might include someone you would love to hire.

Ultimately, knowing your school's purpose and being able to communicate that purpose with genuine enthusiasm will attract people who will want to work alongside you. On the other hand, unclear priorities will result in a revolving door of staff who move on due to frustration or a desire to work toward a clearer purpose. A false facade is likely to result eventually in employee resentment and departure. Be you, but know you. As you interact with others, *be* yourself, but *know* yourself by taking the time to clarify your understanding of your purpose as a school leader.

## Empathy Episode

Read the following Empathy Episode and imagine what it would feel like to be in the teacher's position. Then use the reflection questions to consider leadership blind spots and how to remedy them.

> After teaching at the same school for the past 10 years, you're relocating 500 miles away to accommodate your spouse's new job. During a recent house-hunting

visit, you ask your real estate agent about the local schools. His kids attend private schools, and he shares negative stories about student behavior and about friends who are teachers and have quit the local public schools. You don't know anyone who works in these schools, and you aren't sure how to connect with someone who could answer your questions.

The school you're leaving serves multilanguage learners, families experiencing poverty, and a student population that consists of a majority of students of color. You'd like to find a similar school in your new community. You visit local school websites and find images of mascots, pictures of school exteriors, information about start times and dismissal times, mission and vision statements, and even dress codes. Based on the websites, most of the schools appear to be similar. Despite your research, you can't get much information and can't distinguish one school from another. You complete the district's employment application but wonder how you will ever find a school community like the one you've poured your heart into for the last 10 years.

## Reflection Questions

- What is not being communicated to the prospective candidate in the scenario?
- What can prospective candidates learn about *your* school from your school website?

This scenario demonstrates the importance of communicating a clear school identity for a prospective employment candidate. As noted, a school's identity encompasses its values, mission, and overall culture. The teacher in the scenario has a clear sense of purpose, but she can't determine if she would be a good match for any of the schools in the district or if their identities relate to her personal and professional aspirations. A school with a clearly communicated identity will be more appealing to individuals seeking a workplace where they can contribute meaningfully and align their personal goals with the school's mission. Furthermore, a candidate will appreciate the ability to get a sense of the school environment in terms of how it addresses employees' needs.

From the viewpoint of a prospective employee, these needs may include having a comfortable and safe workspace where people feel secure in their job. In addition, a sense of belonging and connection with colleagues and students is essential for creating a positive work environment. Recognition, appreciation, and opportunities for professional growth and development all contribute to employees' ability to grow in their career and enjoy a fulfilling and productive work experience. All of these factors can be communicated through a well-designed school website.

## How Will You Commit?

- What strategies from this chapter are you committed to implementing?
- Who can help you implement these strategies?
- What outcome do you want to see as a result of implementing these strategies?

## Summary

In this chapter, we asked you to consider who you are as a school leader, to establish a clear school identity, to be able to tell your school's story effectively, and to develop ways to share your school's identity with the community. Further, we addressed how clarity around your individual and institutional purpose and identity sets you up to invite others to join you on your journey, which we will address in Chapter 2.

# 2

# Inviting Excellence

*When I arrived at the interview, there was a complete lack of procedure. It was obvious two [people] on the committee had never seen my résumé. I immediately launched into the lesson to meet their stringent guidelines. I asked a few questions, but it was obvious they were done with me. I was actually glad when I did not get it, thinking what the job itself would have looked like based on the total lack of support and care during the interview.*

—Teacher

It's been said that an interview is like a first date. You're nervous and want to make a good impression. But too often we focus only on the performance of the applicant during the interview and ignore the other side of the table. The interview experience can have a huge effect on whether an individual chooses to accept a position. Interactions with the hiring committee, nonverbal and verbal, convey the values of the school's leadership and the school as a whole. This chapter explores how to optimize interactions so that qualified candidates will choose your school over every other option.

Begin by defining your goals for recruitment and the interview process. If your interview consists only of questions to determine if someone is the best fit for the role at your school, you may be underestimating the impact of the interview experience on the candidate. Recognize that the candidate will leave the interview with impressions about your school and your leadership that they may share with other potential candidates and community stakeholders. We caution you not to discount the ripple effect these communications can have.

Figure 2.1 contains a self-assessment of the interview process at your school. Respond to the statements and reflect on your responses. If you strongly agree with the statement that every interviewee offered a position at your school accepts it, congratulations! It's likely that you have a compelling school culture, and the interview experience closes the deal. If that's not the case, consider what parts of the interview experience might have led candidates to have reservations. They applied and were interested. What happened that changed their mind? How can you find out? How do you know what candidates' impressions are of your school and your leadership? Have you ever talked with the school community stakeholders about how they can informally assist with recruiting top talent to your school?

As you consider how best to conduct the interview process, focus on what you hope candidates say after interacting with you and learning about your school, regardless of whether they're selected for the position. Think about how to design the interview or recruitment experience to elicit such responses regarding aspects of your school.

## Recruitment Fairs

Recruitment fairs, in which multiple employers are brought together with multiple job seekers for convenience and expediency, can be an efficient hiring tactic. They also provide excellent opportunities to increase your school's brand recognition and meet prospective candidates. Most recruitment fairs are held on college campuses, where schools try to snag graduating teacher candidates, or within a specific district, where schools try to convince educators that their school is the one to work with.

One hitch, however, is that such events are often characterized by awkwardness and uncertainty on both sides of the encounter. In a sea of possibilities, how can you make your school stand out? Knowing your audience will help you determine how you approach educators and invite them to apply for your positions.

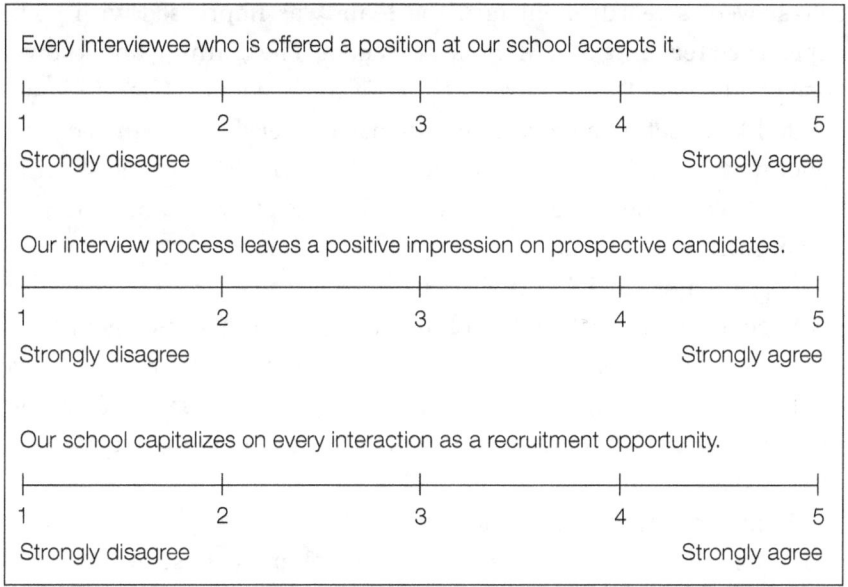

FIGURE 2.1

**School Interview Process Self-Assessment**

After her first year of teaching, Jessica relocated to a new area. The local school district held a recruitment fair in the spring for open positions in the fall. She registered for the event and made travel arrangements, including taking a personal day from the teaching position she held at the time. But the experience was a confusing one. She was given only minimal information about the date, time, and location of the fair. She arrived with a folder full of résumés to a haphazard setup: a room full of tables staffed by people from schools that had openings, but no way to get more information about those positions. A few schools offered brief interviews on the spot, and Jessica completed one with a middle school. Weeks went by without any communication until she got a call offering her a position with that school. She remembers wondering what made her memorable. Was it her résumé? Her responses in the brief interview? The outfit she wore? She never found out.

It's less than ideal to initiate an employment relationship with such uncertainty. To lay a foundation for a more positive hiring experience, recognize the importance of sharing why you're following up with candidates. For example, you can say, "During our conversation at last week's recruitment fair, the team was impressed with your experience teaching at a Montessori school. The training and knowledge you have in this area would benefit our students. Therefore, we would like to set up a more comprehensive interview." Transparency about why a candidate is appealing builds trust. Naming and sharing why they could be a good fit provides feedback to the candidate and communicates the needs and priorities of the school.

To gain more insight into how to improve the interview process at your school, collaborate with organizations holding recruitment fairs (e.g., local colleges or universities) to solicit feedback from candidates on their interview experiences. Identify what educators want from the interview process to create a more rewarding and attractive recruitment process.

Remember that every table at a recruitment fair presents a decision for candidates to stop or pass. As you plan for these events, consider what features of your presentation would be inviting from the candidates' point of view.

Imagine two tables set up next to each other in a high school gym. The first table is dressed with an attractive tablecloth, with school brochures arranged on top. A collage of pictures from the school year is posted on the nearby wall, and school representatives stand nearby, all wearing shirts sporting the school logo and colors. These representatives have a plan: They engage people by talking about their students and school community, they're attentive, and they politely keep people moving so they can speak to as many candidates as possible. The second table has no tablecloth, no backdrop, no handouts, and no personalization. The one school representative who is present spends more time staring at their cell phone than looking around to engage with candidates. This school's lack of attention and preparation telegraphs their lack of a plan. Which table is going to attract candidates?

Inviting Excellence • 27

We've developed a technique called STARS of GOLD (see Figure 2.2) to help you optimize your school's recruitment fair experiences.

FIGURE 2.2
---
**STARS of GOLD**

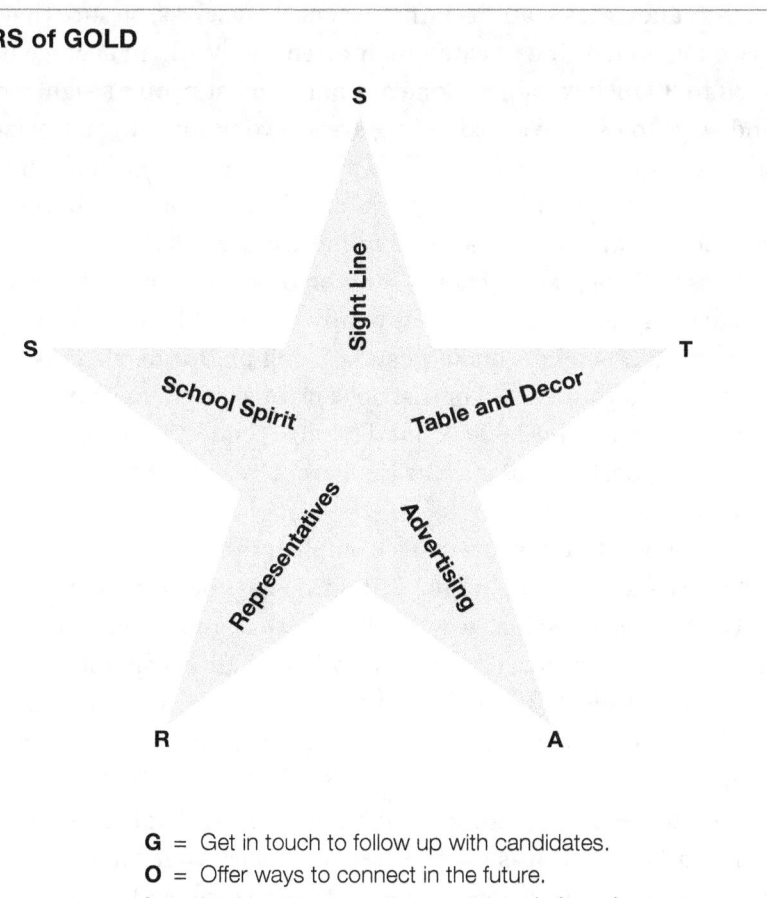

G = Get in touch to follow up with candidates.
O = Offer ways to connect in the future.
L = Look over prospective candidates' résumés.
D = Decide on next steps.

## Reach for the STARS

A well-designed table and surrounding space can draw people to you during a recruitment fair and leave a lasting impression. You want to create a positive experience for candidates, not just exchange information. Use the STARS mnemonic—attending to *S*ight line, *T*able and decor, Advertising, Representatives, and School spirit—to design a setting that makes candidates want to join your faculty.

### Sight line

As candidates scan the fair to orient themselves, be sure that your space has something to catch their attention. With an average height of 28 to 30 inches, tables alone are not in most people's sight line, so find ways to use the surrounding area to your advantage. Horizontal or vertical banners are a great way to capture attention, and they can be secured with temporary hooks or adhesives. Go beyond just the school name and logo to communicate what the school values, expressed through the school's mission or vision statement or images of learning in action. If professionally designed banners are beyond your budget, you can make posters using platforms such as Canva. Tapping into your school or district's print shop (if you have one) can help keep costs affordable. You might also request funding from community support groups such as the Parent Teacher Association (PTA) or local nonprofits.

A handcrafted display can accomplish the same goal of intersecting with candidates' sight line. Trifold displays or foam boards provide a sturdy (and reusable) way to display text and images. Use paint, stickers, bulletin board trim, and other readily available resources to make the display visually appealing. Having students create the display can demonstrate how students are involved in promoting their school.

It may seem like a minor point, but having school representatives stand rather than sit is another way to ensure your table is in candidates' sight line. If the event is long, take turns standing to make eye contact and invite people to your table with a welcoming smile.

### Table and decor

Do not underestimate the power of presentation. The appearance of the table itself conveys a sense of the effort your school is willing to put forth to attract attendees. A poorly arranged table may tell prospective candidates that you don't consider the event worth your time and preparation and may deter candidates from stopping to engage in a conversation. Again, it may seem like a minor point, but even a tablecloth can make a difference, especially if it's covering a table that shows signs of wear and tear. A plastic tablecloth will work, but cloth—in school colors—is best. Next, consider what will be on the table and how it will be arranged. The display should not only look appealing but also be functional. What items do you need within reach to share with candidates? Are there materials for candidates to "grab and go"? Another consideration is table decor. A centerpiece that cultivates curiosity can attract visitors and create an opportunity for you to share information. This could be a student-made artifact of learning, a piece of school history, an interactive game (digital or analog), or a video of the school—anything that will draw people to your space to learn more. Ultimately, the table speaks loudly, so curate what you want it to say.

### *Advertising*

Perhaps the most frequently asked question at a recruitment fair is "Do you have any current openings?" Find a way to clearly articulate the answer upfront so candidates don't have to ask, which can be particularly frustrating in a crowd. For example, display a poster or smaller document that lists current openings and explains how interested candidates can learn about future ones. Another option is a video loop with hiring and job inquiry information. A third option is a postcard with an image of the school or school logo on one side and a QR code linking to job postings and school contact information on the other. Your display should also include information about district-level benefits, licensure, and application processes.

Make it easy for prospective candidates to share résumés and for you and other school representatives to take notes. Jessica has seen a leader use an accordion folder labeled by content area to sort and store résumés quickly at a recruitment fair. Another leader used a three-ring binder with dividers. Devise a system before the event that will facilitate post-event follow-up.

Recruitment fairs are a prime opportunity to advertise your school's purpose and values. You want to be desirable to candidates to fill not only your school's current needs but also openings in the future. Remember that candidates may share their impression of the school with others, which can be an informal, indirect recruitment method in itself. Looking ahead, today's candidates may even be parents of future candidates.

### *Representatives*

Pick the best representative of your school. Think creatively as you consider possibilities among teachers, students, and community partners, but also think strategically. Who can be most effective in telling your story and inviting educators to join your staff? Ensure that those representing your school know why they were selected, understand the goals and expectations, and are trained to communicate effectively. Do not make assumptions or leave anything to chance. A recruitment fair requires initiating conversations, asking genuine questions, and sharing compelling information, so you want to choose people who thrive in a social environment.

Be aware of generational and situational differences. Current graduates may have different priorities than the ones held by veteran staff members years ago. Recent graduates and career switchers will have unique concerns and differing ideas on what constitutes a desirable job. Staff members who have been at your school a long time and get along well with everyone internally may not necessarily have the skills to connect with and attract potential applicants. They may have forgotten what it feels like to be a new graduate or new to an area. On the other hand, they may be the best people to represent your school because they have a deep understanding of its mission. It's up to you to consider these factors and make the best choice.

### *School spirit*

Always have a takeaway item that demonstrates your school spirit for anyone who walks past your table. All that merchandise we talked about in Chapter 1 is useful here. Less expensive items such as stickers, keychains, and pencils can be offered to all visitors. More expensive items such as shirts, bags, and mugs can be reserved to be given in response to particularly promising conversations with candidates. Be creative and unique with these school spirit items to make your school memorable—one example would be fortune cookies with customized messages created by students or staff. Reusable items will bring the school to the forefront of candidates' minds every time they use them. Conventional school spirit takeaways work, but consider ways to customize them so that your school stands out from the crowd.

Keep the design or theme of your recruitment table and its surroundings universally appealing. Does it speak to individuals across generations? We sometimes assume that others have the same knowledge base or interests as we do. To relate to all prospective candidates, test your assumptions by asking yourself, "How would this person know about _____? Why would this person care about it?" For example, if you make friendship bracelets your takeaway item under the impression that everyone is a Taylor Swift fan, your booth may be Pinterest-worthy, but it may not actually further the goal of connecting with prospective candidates who might follow other musical trends. Consider who might feel disconnected from the theme or takeaway.

## Go for GOLD

Recruitment events are a golden opportunity to connect with prospective candidates. Here are some actions to take to "go for GOLD" after recruitment events or individual interactions:

- **Get in touch to follow up with candidates.** Send a timely email thanking them for connecting during the event. Include information on the school and a reminder of how to access job postings.
- **Offer ways to connect in the future.** In the follow-up email, share information about other recruitment fairs and school events that are open to the public, or invite candidates to follow the school's social media accounts.
- **Look over prospective candidates' résumés.** Record details about your interactions while they're fresh in your mind. If you did not attend the event, debrief with the school representatives and make notes.

- **Decide on next steps.** Based on the résumés and impressions gained from interactions, you and others involved in the decision-making and hiring process need to decide whether to invite prospective candidates to interview for existing openings.

Using the STARS of GOLD approach to recruitment fair planning and follow-up can lead to positive interactions with prospective candidates. Recruitment fairs are often where candidates get their first impressions of a school, and you want yours to be a desirable choice. Such events also require an investment of time and resources to maximize your school's reach and positive impact.

## Informal Recruitment Opportunities

All of us share the experience of learning about our current workplace for the first time. It's important to remember that each school event can also be an informal opportunity to recruit prospective educators. Don't underestimate the potential of an audience of 500 attending your school musical. It's possible that within that gathering of parents, grandparents, neighbors, relatives, friends, and other fans of your students are some talented, dedicated, well-trained educators. How are you maximizing these informal recruitment opportunities?

Carrie recently attended her niece's musical performance at a local middle/high school. The director exuded pride in the students, expressed gratitude for the support from parents throughout the rehearsals, and spoke of enjoying her job. Carrie had been in other school audiences before, and the contrast was striking. Once, she recalls, the head of the elementary school seemed frustrated with the students, and her words suggested a much different school culture and tone. The impressions Carrie took away from these two encounters lasted long after her niece's performances.

Are you leveraging school events such as musical and theater performances, PTA meetings, family engagement nights, sporting events (both at home and away), and field trips as recruitment opportunities? The number of people who learn about your school from these events over the course of a year could be in the thousands. That's a significant market—and one you don't want to overlook. Although you don't have to announce future openings at these events, what is shared about your school and how the staff interacts with attendees at school functions can affect a future applicant pool.

As the number of applicants from traditional college and university pathways decreases, it's important to expand the very notion of "pathways." It could be that someone attending a school event is considering switching careers or is thinking about going into education. Every interaction is an opportunity to recruit for the school. If the right circumstances arise, don't hesitate to ask, "Have you ever considered education as a career?" This question can serve as a starting point for hiring someone who might qualify for alternative certification licensure or a program such as Teach for America.

## The Interview Process

Schools often face a time crunch to hire new staff and therefore rush the process. Don't let this happen in your school. Invest time in the interview process, keeping in mind that the person you're interviewing could be working at the school for years—decades, even. If a hiring deadline looms, consider how you can streamline the interview process without compromising the integrity of your hiring practices. This could mean strategically scheduling interviews during the school day and providing classroom coverage for members of the interview team or reducing the number of questions asked in each interview so that you have time to engage with more candidates.

Ask yourself, "Is an in-person interview mandatory?" This question crops up more frequently than in the pre-COVID era. The benefits of an in-person interview include the opportunity to assess the candidate's nonverbal communication and the ability for the candidate to visit the school firsthand—including the waiting area, which can leverage appealing displays to inspire or inform candidates. Online interviews, on the other hand, eliminate travel expenses for the interviewee, avoid possibly awkward interactions among candidates visiting the school at the same time, and allow for the use of artificial intelligence (AI) assistants to take notes.

Regardless of format, being prompt about interview start and end times conveys respect for all parties involved. If additional time is needed, you can schedule another meeting or ask the interviewee to send an email to share their remaining thoughts and resolve any uncertainties or unaddressed questions.

Another thing to consider is who will conduct the interview. Will you, as the school leader, be the only interviewer, or will you choose a team? If the interview is conducted by a team, those who serve on the team should have a vested interest in the outcome. They need to genuinely care about who gets hired, especially if they may end up working closely with them. Selecting an interview team made up of members who will directly collaborate with the new hire ensures that the interview process is not only thorough but also aligned with the needs and dynamics of the existing team. In addition, including staff members who are in the leadership pipeline, even if they are not going to be a direct collaborator, helps them grow in this skillset.

## Preparing the Team for Interviews

It's important to design the interview process carefully so that it's both efficient and productive. Assuming you're using a team of interviewers, preparation should include the following steps:

1. *Set expectations* for the team, including that each person can clearly articulate the school's vision, mission, and values.
2. *Determine the role each team member will play* during the interview.
3. *Review all questions* and know which ones each team member will ask.
4. *Come to a consensus* about the qualities of an ideal candidate.
5. *Review the candidate's résumé* as a group.
6. *Explain the method for taking notes* or rating responses.

Team preparation should include a review of the school's vision, mission, and values to ensure that candidates receive consistent messages. Every team member should be able to clearly articulate those elements of school culture through stories that stick and answers to candidate questions.

It's also essential to be transparent about the details of the decision-making process with all team members. This includes how the interview process will be conducted, how input will be gathered and considered, and who will ultimately make the final decision (i.e., the team as a whole or the school leaders). Establishing these details early on ensures that everyone understands their role and the significance of their input to the process. Executive decisions may be necessary for a variety of reasons, such as the principal learning additional information from the candidate's references or the first-choice candidate not accepting the position. Some of this information may not be appropriate or reasonable to share with the entire team. School leaders can communicate the need to pivot without divulging details that may not align with human resources policies.

The roles of team members must be clearly defined. Will they ask questions, take notes, or just listen? There are various ways to approach this. One is to have one interviewer ask the question and listen to understand while the others take notes on the response. This option allows the person asking the question to maintain eye contact and focus on the response. It alleviates the stress of listening, demonstrating interest, and taking notes simultaneously. Team members can take turns asking questions. Another approach is to record the interview so that no one has to take notes, and everyone can focus on engaging with the applicant. Recording the interaction also allows the interviewers to review the session later so they can base their decisions on a correct understanding of what the interviewee said.

Developing substantive interview questions or prompts is one of the most important tasks in the interview process. Agreeing on the prompts and deciding who will present each one (in the case of multiple questioners) are essential. It's important to consider how the interview questions address the values and priorities of the school—and what candidates' responses can reveal about their suitability for the job. A well-designed interview will ensure that the selected individual possesses the skills the school is looking for and is committed to the core principles that define the school's identity. See Figure 2.3 for a sample of interview prompts that can uncover relevant qualities in prospective staff.

**FIGURE 2.3**

**Interview Prompts**

| Category | Prompt | What the Candidate's Response Reveals |
|---|---|---|
| Mission, vision, and values | Describe how your teaching methods align with our school's mission, vision, and values. | • Understanding of the school's mission, vision, and values<br>• Knowledge of teaching methods<br>• Depth of understanding of teaching practice<br>• Connection between their instructional choices and the school culture |
| Teaching philosophy | Describe an effective lesson you've recently taught and how it reflects your personal teaching philosophy. | • What they believe constitutes an effective lesson<br>• How they measure effectiveness<br>• Whether their decisions are teacher-focused or student-focused<br>• Beliefs about students and about teaching as a profession |
| Classroom management | A student continuously disrupts instruction by blurting out, tapping, getting out of their seat, and making noises. Their off-task behavior is interfering with the learning of other students. How would you address the situation while maintaining a positive and inclusive environment for all students? | • Knowledge of strategies for addressing common disruptive student behavior<br>• The nature of their relationships with students<br>• Policies for communication with families<br>• Ability to assess whether actions are likely to de-escalate or escalate a situation |
| Community engagement | How do you engage with colleagues, parents, and the broader community to enhance the educational experience for all students? | • Comfort level and experience working with stakeholders<br>• Professionalism<br>• Willingness to network<br>• Whether the partnerships they build are superficial or substantive |
| Collaboration | Describe a time when you successfully collaborated with colleagues. What made the experience successful? | • Understanding of collaboration<br>• Their criteria for successful collaboration<br>• Whether they are student-focused collaborative interactions<br>• Conflict resolution experience |

| Category | Prompt | What the Candidate's Response Reveals |
|---|---|---|
| Professional development | Describe a recent professional development experience. How did it contribute to your continuous growth as an educator? | • Self-awareness in identifying areas for growth<br>• Attitude toward continuous improvement and professional growth<br>• Ability to implement new learning<br>• Ability to connect professional growth to student outcomes |
| Investing in self | What is an area in which you would like to grow? Why are you interested in learning more about this area? How could you achieve your goal? | • Desire for personal growth<br>• Ability to self-advocate<br>• Ability to identify an area or new path for growth<br>• Plans for implementation |

Reviewing the candidate's résumé as a team provides an opportunity to ensure that everyone has familiarity with the candidate's background and experience, thereby avoiding the possibility that a team member will ask a question that's already answered on the résumé, which is an obvious waste of time. Before looking at résumés, however, the team should agree on what it means to be a qualified candidate for the open position. That means ensuring ahead of time that everyone has roughly the same characteristics in mind when they visualize an "ideal candidate." When conducting interviews, it's crucial to identify and prioritize the criteria that matter most for the position. The team should engage in a discussion about the relative importance of various qualifications and attributes. For example, if you have a departmentalized 3rd grade team that already includes team members with strengths in math and science, you will be looking for someone whose strengths are in literacy to balance out the team. By clearly identifying and agreeing on the key priorities beforehand, the team can ensure that the evaluation process is aligned with the specific needs of the school and the position.

Making a plan for rating or scoring the candidate is also essential. A simple rating scale to assess the candidate's response to each interview question might look like this:

1 = Insufficient response
2 = Sufficient response
3 = Robust response

Some of these pre-interview activities may seem mundane. However, taking a transparent, principled approach to preparation and clearly outlining expectations safeguards the integrity of the hiring process.

> **Try This: Rapid Interview Prep for Your Team**
>
> When time is tight, school leaders can prepare their interview team in less than 10 minutes by following these key steps:
>
> 1. *Set clear expectations* by quickly reviewing the school's vision, mission, and values to ensure consistent messaging.
> 2. *Assign specific roles* to each team member. Who will ask questions? Take notes? Focus on observing responses?
> 3. *Briefly discuss* the candidate's résumé and the key qualities you're looking for, ensuring everyone agrees on what makes an ideal candidate.
>
> This streamlined approach ensures a focused and effective interview process.

## Preparing the Candidate for the Interview

In addition to preparing the interview team, it's important to prepare the interviewee. When you extend an invitation to a prospective candidate, either firsthand or through an administrative assistant, go beyond basic information such as time, date, and location to communicate your expectations for the process, including interview questions (see Figure 2.4 for an example). This invitation is an opportunity to make a favorable first (or second, if you're following up a recruitment event) impression. Candidates may have multiple offers, so you want the invitation, as well as the interview process itself, to have positive associations.

An invitation should feel different from a list of instructions. To keep candidates excited about the possibility of joining your school, be sure to use warm and enthusiastic language in your communication. The invitation should include basics such as date and time, parking

**FIGURE 2.4**

**Sample Interview Invitation**

***Empowering Students***

***Creating Leaders***

You are invited to join us for an interview at
Poplar Hill Elementary School

June 21, 2023, at 3:00 PM
1199 First Street
Tillsburg, Alabama

Park in the visitors' spots located in the school's lower lot on Corner Street. Enter the building using the Corner Street entrance. Look for the orange pawprints to find your way.

**Bring one lesson plan and be prepared to answer the questions in the attached document.**

Learn more about our school:
www.poplarhilles.k12.org

RSVP to Mrs. Atwood at (205) 555-5555

details, how to enter the building, what to bring, and any other relevant information. For example, if cars often block the school entrance at a certain time, you might suggest arriving a bit earlier.

Including interview questions in the invitation is a way to reduce the anxiety candidates may feel ahead of time. An interview should not come across as an opportunity for "gotcha moments," when an interviewer uses tricky questions to fluster a candidate. Some people are good at responding on the spot, and others need time to process. It's also worth noting that some people have physical responses such as sweating or flushing when experiencing stress or anxiety, which can add another layer of distraction for the interviewee. Including the interview questions in the invitation makes it more likely that candidates will be able to respond with their best thoughts, not tainted with nervous energy. As researchers Feiler and Powell (2016) explain, "We found that anxious interviewees on average appeared less inter-personally warm and assertive (as rated by external raters) and received lower ratings of interview performance" (p. 14). This finding suggests that school leaders may be less likely to hire someone, even if that person is otherwise qualified, based on a perceived lack of competence and confidence that stems from expressions of anxiety. Removing possible stressors, including those related to expectations (and logistics, as described earlier), creates a more equitable experience for interviewees and likely will yield better outcomes for all parties. Providing interview questions in advance primes candidates to give their best responses and helps create transparency about the qualifications and characteristics the ideal candidate should possess to ensure everyone is on the same page.

### Conducting the Interview

After you've prepared for the interview and sent your carefully crafted invitation, it's time for the interview itself.

As noted, you want to leave the candidate with a positive impression of the school. Be sure the candidate is greeted by a secretary or other designated person and escorted to the interview location. Offering water, coffee, or tea is a hospitable gesture.

When asking questions—and throughout the interview—all members of the team should give the candidate their undivided attention. That attention includes noticing nonverbal communication and body language used by all parties and any tension that may arise. The interview is also an opportunity to share relevant information about the school, including what type of support and onboarding new faculty members receive. Such support might include mentorship or districtwide initiatives. Providing a handout that communicates the school's mission, vision, and values (even if these have already been communicated) reinforces the message the school wants to convey; the handout may include examples of what the mission and vision look like in action or highlight the type of interpersonal connections the school fosters, as indicated, for example, by teachers attending school sporting events. Showcasing the school's sense of community and connection can give the candidate an idea of what it would be like to work at the school and spark enthusiasm. If possible, take the candidate on a tour of the school building to give them an even better sense of the school's culture and the ability to picture themselves as part of the community.

At the same time, it's important to be careful not to lead anyone on or make promises that cannot be kept. By being transparent and honest during the interview process, both the interviewer and the interviewee can establish trust and respect for each other, ultimately resulting in a more positive hiring experience. Even if the candidate is ultimately not selected, a good interview experience can leave a lasting impression they may share with others.

## Completing Post-Interview Tasks

The end of the interview isn't the end of the process. The first post-interview task is to debrief the experience with the team. As noted earlier, it is essential to have a plan for how the interviewers will rate or score the candidate. Each team member should determine their individual score before sharing as a group so that people aren't influenced by others' scores. The debriefing process is equally important. Team members should listen to each other's comments respectfully and handle any significant disagreements constructively.

Given the reality that the schedule often doesn't allow sufficient time to debrief between interviews, consider having all team members enter their scores and notes into a shared Google Form. This preserves everyone's initial impressions with a quick data capture. Later, you can hold a longer debrief conversation about all applicants. If you prefer to debrief after each interview, schedule appointments at large enough intervals to allow for adequate discussion time. Averaging team members' scores can provide an initial way to compare candidates and guide further discussion about next steps.

Traditionally, interviewees are expected to send a thank-you note or email after the interview, but it's worth noting that the candidates dedicate time and effort to participate in interviews—perhaps even more so than the interviewers. With that in mind, we suggest sending a follow-up email to the candidates. A simple "thank you" can have a tremendous impact because it acknowledges the prospect's contributions and value. The note should also explain the next steps in the process, even if you shared them at the end of the interview; it never hurts to repeat them. Including this information can reduce the candidate's post-interview stress and answer questions they may have thought of after the interview. No one should have to spend days wondering how the interview went and worrying about what to do next. See Figure 2.5 for an example of a follow-up email.

**FIGURE 2.5**

**Sample Follow-Up Email**

> Dear *[applicant name]*,
>
> Thank you for participating in an interview at *[school]*. It was a pleasure to meet you and learn more about your passion and skills. The next steps in the process are *[include the process of notification, estimated timeline, and who to expect communication from]*.
>
> In the meantime, you are welcome to stay connected with our school by visiting our school website *[insert link]* and our social media sites *[insert links to X, Instagram, YouTube, etc.]*. Attached is a pamphlet about our school and a Frequently Asked Questions document that may address any lingering questions.
>
> Kind regards,
>
> *[principal name]*

In addition to leaving a positive impression on a candidate, a follow-up email can keep the door open for future interactions even if the person is not hired. People tend to remember how they felt in a particular situation. Design the interview experience so that they would welcome another interaction with you and your school.

## Consequences

Interview experiences can have both intended and unintended consequences. Here's an example of an unintended consequence:

> A high-performing school with an opening in the math department recruits and sets up an interview with one of the top math teachers in the district. The teacher currently commutes over 30 minutes to and from their school but lives just 5 minutes from the school in need of a teacher, so a successful hire feels like a sure thing. What could possibly go wrong?
>
> When the teacher arrived, however, the principal, excited about a strong, highly effective teacher, just assumed the teacher wanted and would take the job. Over the course of the interview, the principal shared her struggles with the current negative culture at the school and the challenges she'd been experiencing since taking the reins four years prior. She spoke disparagingly about some of her teachers, parents, and school staff. These revelations were alarming to the candidate. The more comfortable the principal became, the more she shared—and the more she scared off the candidate.
>
> As the teacher left the interview, she called a friend who teaches at the school and confided that, if offered the position, she would not accept it. She said, "I would love the shorter commute, and it would make a lot of sense. But the issues with the school culture really scare me. It's worth the drive to be somewhere I know I am happy and work with a leader I trust." In this case, the teacher's long commute may have presented an obstacle, but it was nothing compared to the prospect of immersion in a negative school culture.

Although the principal was honest about the struggle the school was having with culture, when she began speaking negatively about teachers, she revealed herself to be part of the problem. Ultimately, she deterred a candidate who wanted the same thing the principal wanted: a positive school culture. The unintended consequence of the interview experience was discouraging a promising and highly desirable candidate.

In another example of unintended consequences, a teacher shared the experience of her very first interview, for a middle school teaching position in 8th grade math. After she had answered one or two questions, the principal essentially told her that she was too young for the job; nevertheless, she persisted, sharing her collegiate portfolio with the interviewer. She didn't get the job. In relating the incident, the teacher describes it as the most deflating experience she had as a new college graduate, and she has replayed and shared it numerous times. (She earned a job at the very next school she interviewed with.) Because she works and lives in the same community as the school that rejected her, it's possible that her repeated recounting of her experience may be leading others to view the school in a negative light—a consequence that the principal would surely be dismayed to learn about.

The lesson here is to be aware of the possibility of an interview's unintended consequences and to minimize them. Specifically, be mindful of the following:

- Oversharing can lead to revealing weaker areas of the school culture or operations that may deter candidates who could be part of the solution.
- Unclear or lack of communication can lead to misperceptions and misunderstandings.
- Making promises can lead a candidate to have unrealistic expectations and eventual "buyer's remorse."
- Rushing through an interview can be interpreted by the candidate as disinterest or disrespect.
- Sarcasm, informal comments, or even well-intended humor can come across as rude or inappropriate and cause candidates to reconsider working at the school.

In contrast to these experiences and caveats, a well-designed interview process can have positive, intended consequences. Kathryn Lemerich, a STEM supervisor, reflected on a recent interview:

> In my final interview for a vice principal position, which I enthusiastically accepted, I vividly remember two things about the interview. The first was the personality, kindness, and character of the principal I would be working for. I remember he asked about my interests outside of work and followed it up with the value he places on work–life balance. His interactions and this question told me a lot about the type of

leadership and the culture I would be walking into. It felt like a great fit. The second was the responses of the interview committee members to the question "What do you love most about this school?" Listening to the teachers talk about how wonderful the students are, the support they have, the programs they are able to develop, and how the school "feels like a family" was all I needed to hear to know this felt like home.

Kate's reflection emphasizes the importance of the principal's verbal and nonverbal communication and of the responses from committee members to her question.

As a school leader, you represent your school; every interaction is an opportunity to cultivate positive feelings toward your school community. Even when you know a candidate is not the best fit for the position, assume they're going to talk to at least three people about their experience. What do you want them to say?

## Empathy Episode

Read the following Empathy Episode and imagine what it would feel like to be in the teacher's position. Then use the reflection questions to consider leadership blind spots and how to remedy them.

> You've just relocated to a new area and have landed a job interview at an elementary school. The email you received gave the time and date but no other information. The interview is tomorrow at 10:00 a.m. You accept the invitation but will have to find a sitter on short notice to stay with your two children.
>
> You arrive at the school early so that you have a buffer if you get lost or stuck in traffic. You push the buzzer to be let into the building. No answer. You wait. After five minutes, you press it again. No answer. You dig out your cell phone and send an email notifying the recipient that you are outside the school. Ugh! You were early, but now you're late and sweating in the heat.
>
> Finally, someone is leaving the building, and the door opens. You make your way inside and find the main office. Walking in, you notice two other people waiting. The principal comes out, calls a name, and goes back into a room without even acknowledging your presence. Your stomach drops. You feel unseen and frustrated at the work you had to do just to get inside the building. The other person waiting with you shares that the interviews are about an hour behind schedule. Anxiety swells since you asked the sitter to stay for only an hour. Now you're frantically texting the sitter and apologizing. Frustration is brewing and you haven't even gotten to the interview. Now you're thinking, *Maybe I should just go home.*

### Reflection Questions

- How could the interview experience have been improved for this candidate?
- What do you think prospective candidates learn about your school from their interview experience?

As this scenario illustrates, neglecting to strategically plan the candidate's interview experience is a missed opportunity to make a great first impression. Including only limited information in the invitation left a lot of unknowns. The uncertainty added to the candidate's stress, and we know that people can't be their best selves if they're stressed. Not explaining how to enter the building or having someone available to greet the interviewee caused additional stress. Being expected to sit in a waiting area with no welcome or acknowledgment felt disrespectful and did not create a friendly environment. A far better approach would include a greeting such as this: "I'm so glad you accepted our invitation to interview. Thank you for arriving on time." With the interview schedule running behind, ignoring the delay was also inconsiderate. An apology and an offer to reschedule would have been appropriate.

Making an effort to reduce stress and create positive environments for candidates acknowledges the validity of Maslow's hierarchy of needs, ensuring safety, creating a sense of belonging, and promoting self-esteem and self-actualization in candidates. As you review the suggestions and recommendations in this chapter, consider how your school and you as a school leader are meeting these needs. For example, you can address physiological needs by ensuring that the interview environment includes a comfortable chair, access to water, and, if the interview is lengthy, appropriate breaks. Providing clear information ahead of time about the interview process, expectations, parking, traffic, and next steps can help create a sense of predictability and security, addressing safety needs and reducing anxiety so that candidates can focus on their performance. Creating a welcoming and inclusive environment during the interview fosters a sense of belonging, and positive interactions with interviewers and staff can contribute to a feeling of connection with the potential workplace community. Acknowledging and appreciating the candidate's achievements, skills, and experiences in the interview addresses self-esteem. Feedback that highlights their strengths can boost confidence and self-worth. Discussion about the candidate's aspirations, career goals, and how these align with the position and the organization's mission tap into self-actualization needs. Opportunities for professional growth and contributing to meaningful work are integral to this level on the hierarchy. By considering these aspects, interviewers can assess a candidate's qualifications in the context of a positive and holistic interview experience that benefits both sides of the exchange.

## How Will You Commit?

- What strategies from this chapter are you committed to implementing?
- Who can help you implement these strategies?
- What outcome do you want to see as a result of implementing these strategies?

## Summary

In this chapter, we examined how to invite potential candidates to work at your school and how to design an interview process that benefits both the candidates and the institution. By intentionally designing a process that leads to a positive experience, the school is more likely to hire staff who can advance the school's mission, vision, and goals. Successful interviews create a positive first impression and establish a strong foundation for the process of joining the school's faculty, which is the topic of Chapter 3.

# 3

# Welcoming New Team Members

*Having mentors or colleagues in different roles who have been specifically pointed out or assigned to support me (and other new folks) has been super helpful. No one knows all the workings of a school building, so knowing that there are multiple people with different skill sets and knowledge who are there for me eased anxiety.*

—Jennifer Orr, teacher

Creating a welcoming environment for new teachers is crucial for their success and satisfaction with their new schools. Jennifer's statement highlights the importance of supportive colleagues. However, it's not enough to assign mentors and expect them and others to do all the work. School leaders also need to assess the effectiveness of the processes for welcoming and onboarding new hires, which includes evaluating whether new teachers feel a sense of belonging and support structures are adequate. The goal is to create an environment where new teachers feel supported, valued, and empowered to contribute to the school's mission and purpose. Use the self-assessment tool in Figure 3.1 to reflect on how your school currently welcomes new team members.

**FIGURE 3.1**

**Welcoming New Hires Self-Assessment**

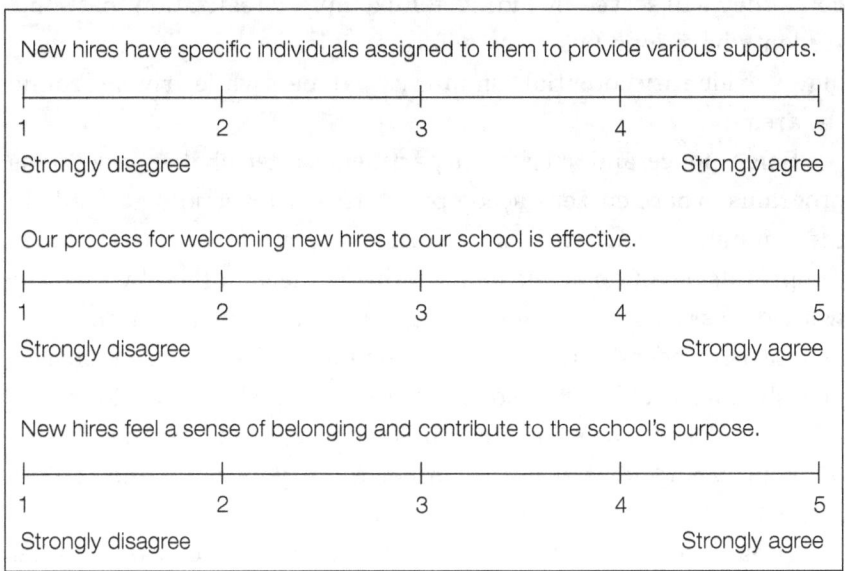

## The Welcoming Process

Welcoming new teachers to a school is a critical aspect for ensuring their smooth transition and integration into the school community. One way to get off to a good start is to give each new staff member a welcome kit, perhaps including a note written by students and one or more school spirit items, such as a school shirt or lanyard. Consider asking your school's PTA to collect donations or raise funds to create such kits. Local businesses or chambers of commerce may also be interested in helping.

The welcome kit should also include useful information such as a list of neighborhood eateries; nearby medical, banking, postal, and other services; and daycare or senior living facilities. A printed copy of the employee handbook (or a QR code for easy digital access) is another good item for new staff to have. In addition, because knowing important members of the local community can be helpful, consider including a handout with contact information for school board members, elected officials, and established community partners.

In addition to a welcome kit, a driving or walking tour of the surrounding area can deepen a newcomer's understanding of the students they will serve—including, for example, a realization that some students have long bus rides before arriving at school. Newcomers may also identify potential community partners while driving around the area.

Some police and sheriff's departments offer civilian ride-along programs, where citizens accompany officers responding to calls in the community. Participation in such a program made Carrie realize the prevalence of domestic disputes in the neighborhood where she worked. Jessica also saw some tough situations during a ride-along, helping her understand students' context more deeply and reconsider how she interacted with students. For example, she realized that not all students have the same structure at home, so she began referring to "your caring adult at home" rather than "your mom and dad" to respect students' varied home environments.

Organized social gatherings with school staff can be another important component of the welcoming process. In 1996, Carrie was hired at an elementary school with a long history of very low turnover, so the staff had not had much practice welcoming new members. To herald the addition of two new teachers for the first time in many years, the principal made his expectations clear by organizing a potluck meal before school began. At the gathering, each teacher shared funny stories—many about their own mistakes over the years, which helped Carrie and her fellow newcomer feel safe and reassured that this school was a place where mistakes and learning were normalized. After the meal, the principal asked each teacher, many of whom had taught for close to 30 years, to find some school supplies they had an abundance of and bring them to the upcoming inservice training to give to the two new teachers. The 22-year-olds found themselves nurtured, supported, and equipped with both mentors and supplies.

## Onboarding

Clear communication between the school administration and the new hire is a crucial component of the onboarding process. This includes providing information about school culture, expectations, policies, and any relevant resources and materials needed for the job. Key things to communicate include the first day to report, when the building is open during the summer, and dates for onboarding training or tasks.

Don't underestimate the need to help new staff prepare. Although candidates may not have asked them in the interview, once they accept the position, questions about how they will do their job will undoubtedly arise. New hires may have a surface-level understanding of the job but not a nuanced comprehension of how to *execute* the job. For example, they know that they will be teaching 4th grade but will have questions and require guidance related to the expectations for teaching 4th grade in this specific school. As a school leader, you may want to establish a team to help with this type of onboarding task, but you need to be involved and monitor its effectiveness.

### Who's Who?

Introduce new hires to support staff to help them navigate how to secure resources and learn about policies and procedures. It's all about knowing whom to ask for help when issues or questions arise. Facilitating introductions removes the stress of the new hire having to initiate conversations with people they don't know, and knowing the name of a few staff members creates a sense of security. Introductions can be done before the school year begins or during the first days. One way to create time in the existing schedule for these interactions is to host an "eat and greet lunch" for new hires and the "who's who" staff members, who are primarily office, itinerant, and classified staff. These people provide vital school services, so connecting new hires to them is important. A "who's who" chart like the one in Figure 3.2 makes it easier to remember people's names and responsibilities and know where to find them in the building or how to contact them.

### Where's What?

No matter how small or big your school, or whether a tour was part of the interview experience, offer a tour of the building once the new hire has been finalized. A personalized tour should include specifics for that person's role. If you can't give personalized tours to all new personnel, small-group tours may circumvent the embarrassment of asking questions in a large group. Extend the tour to cover things you might not think to include, such as dumpsters, teacher parking areas, and locations of lifesaving equipment. Don't assume people will figure this out for themselves. Jessica worked at a school for two years before finding out where the cafeteria ice machine was. She was curious about where the other teachers were getting ice but was reluctant to ask.

### FIGURE 3.2

**Sample "Who's Who" Handout**

| Name | Role | Responsibilities | Location |
|---|---|---|---|
| [Name and picture] | Bookkeeper | Oversees payroll, time cards, fundraisers, keys to rooms | [Room location/ number] |
| [Name and picture] | Lead custodian | Handles daily custodial duties, spills, and accidents | [Room location/ number] Fastest way to locate is using the walkie-talkie |
| [Name and picture] | School security officer | Monitors car line, lunch, and hallways | [Room location/ number] |
| **Other People You May See in Our Building** | | | |
| [Name and picture] | Learning director | Oversees curriculum, instruction, and assessment for a specific grade band | [Email address] |
| [Name and picture] | Instructional technology technician | Troubleshoots issues with technology and internet | [Email address] |
| [Name and picture] | School board member | Oversees the superintendent, approves budget, represents constituents, and discusses policies | [Email address] |

Furnishing new employees with a stand-alone map of the school, with room numbers and common spaces marked, is also helpful. Although most schools include a building map in the faculty handbook, newcomers will appreciate having access to the information before the start of the school year. Remember, the overarching goal is to welcome new hires and reduce stress caused by the unknown or the new.

## Welcome to Your Space

In preparation for new staff, assign rooms and prepare inventory lists so that the new hire knows what furniture and equipment will be provided. Protect vacated rooms from being "picked over" by other staff. It's disheartening to arrive at a new job and find that furniture is missing or that others swapped items. Such behavior isn't a rite of passage; it's stealing.

It's also frustrating to inherit junk and to face a messy classroom. Make sure random papers and trash have been discarded. Having the classroom cleaned out and cleaned up signals that the school cares about the teaching and learning environment. If necessary, ask volunteers from the school's PTA or local businesses to help prepare rooms for new hires. (When using outside volunteers, be sure to remove confidential paperwork such as data reports, demographic information, or contact information from the space.) Let the new teacher know when the room will be available to them. Some districts or schools offer stipends to set up classrooms. If this is an option, inform new hires of the opportunity and explain the process for receiving the stipend. If stipends are unavailable, combine room setup with other onboarding tasks to minimize how often new hires need to come to work before their paid contract time. Also consider having a storage area for new hires to keep supplies until their room is ready.

Keys make people feel secure. Provide keys to the room and any lockable spaces. If the desk drawers and cabinets no longer have keys or cannot be locked, provide a lock or an alternative lockable space. The classroom/office space is where new hires will spend hours every day; it should be a place where they feel comfortable and safe.

Mailboxes, classrooms, and offices should display employee names—accurately—from the beginning. Even if it's handmade for late hires, a nameplate communicates care and is a welcoming touch. And accuracy matters in creating a sense of belonging. When Jessica was a new hire at a school with a high rate of turnover, she found the former teacher's name on the nameplate outside her room. When she asked if she could replace it, an office staff member told her she could "when you work here long enough to get one"—a disheartening response. When asked how long that would be, one of the school leaders replied, "If you make it past your first year." Jessica made her own nameplate and posted it over the existing one. Although she lasted a year at that school, she chose to leave because the culture did not make her feel welcome or valued.

When Carrie asked a new teacher what she could do to help him, he responded, "Can you get this fixed?" and gestured to the nameplate outside the classroom door featuring the previous teacher's name. Carrie quickly came to the rescue by making a new nameplate out of cardstock, but she registered the importance of changing the nameplates and how teachers feel when that simple task is not done. If you have nameplates outside classrooms and in other spaces, be sure they're accurate and up-to-date.

> **Try This: Make a Nameplate**
>
> Creating and posting nameplates in your school may be easier than you realize. They don't need to be elaborate, and there are a number of options for making your own. Remember that nameplates can include additional information, too. Here are some ideas:
>
> - *Hand-crafted nameplate.* Use craft materials such as fabrics, paints, pom-poms, stencils, and stickers to craft nameplates on posterboard, cardboard, or cardstock. Doing this as a team-building activity during a staff inservice session is a fun way to get to know one another.
> - *Fabricated nameplate.* Use technology such as a cutting machine, laser printer, or 3D printer to design and fabricate a nameplate. If you don't have these tools in your building, check with the public library, colleges, or local businesses to see if they have them available for use by your staff. You may even have staff who own these machines and are willing to bring them to school for a designated nameplate-creating activity.

Welcoming New Team Members • 55

- *Digitally designed nameplate.* Use websites or software such as Canva or Google Drawings to design poster-size nameplates. Print on a color printer or use a poster maker, if available.
- *College celebration nameplate.* Display pennants from the colleges and universities staff attended, decorated with staff members' names. A display of this type can connect students with opportunities related to college and careers. This style of nameplate might work best in secondary schools.
- *Favorite book nameplate.* Use a template of a book and display both staff members' names and the title of their favorite book. This kind of display can help support a focus on literacy and encourage students to read.
- *Personality type nameplate.* We'll talk more about personality tests in Chapter 5, but the topic is worth a brief mention here. After staff members complete a personality test or similar activity, add relevant information about their personal qualities that could be useful in building and working in teams to their nameplate (see Figure 3.3 for an example).

FIGURE 3.3

**Sample Personality Nameplate**

**The Adventurer**

"You're a fast learner, able to pick up new skills and juggle different projects and roles with relative ease."

 **Jessica Holloway
Innovation Coach**

https://mycreativetype.com
/type/adventurer/

## Technology

Don't assume that new hires will have a personal device to use at school. If staff are expected to communicate and stay informed via email and other digital communication methods, equipping them with a laptop or similar device is critical. Work with the appropriate departments to provide access to email and information about device login, instructional resource credentials, school Wi-Fi passwords, and other relevant items. Various grants can support districts or schools in purchasing technology. Chromebooks are an affordable alternative to laptops, but be sure that they are able to meet staff's needs before investing in them (for instance, Chromebooks may not be compatible with Microsoft Office or other required software).

Offering a technology training session can reduce stress by enabling new staff—and others—to learn what tools are available and how to use them. Don't assume that people will just figure it out. They might, but they may also get frustrated along the way. Proactive support will reduce stress as new hires adjust to new tools. For example, if classrooms use an Apple TV to connect the teacher's device to the screen, post connection directions on the wall next to the screen and include a QR code that links to a video demonstrating the process. Hold a mini training session to cover email tips, including customizing a signature, adjusting default settings, leveraging settings that are helpful, saving contacts to avoid them being labeled as junk or spam, and using templates for responding efficiently.

**Instructional Materials**

Schedule time to ensure that new hires have access to all curricular resources, digital and physical, and pacing guides. Explain what materials are available and where they're stored. Taking this step is especially important for elementary teachers who use various manipulatives for math and literacy and science teachers who conduct experiments. Related arts or elective teachers, such as those who teach physical education, band, art, or career and technical education courses, require specific resources to meet their standards. It's critical for new hires in these fields to know what learning resources are provided and how they're replenished. New hires who teach students with disabilities or students who are English language learners will require access to individualized education plans (IEPs) and other supporting documentation.

To ensure newcomers have the instructional materials they need, consider these questions: What consumables or administrative supplies are provided to staff? Does the school have a supply closet where these items are kept? Are there funds for copy paper, staples, pencils, and other teaching supplies? It's frustrating for teachers to purchase supplies and later discover that the school provides those supplies at no cost. Providing an inventory of these items communicates what to expect from the school and what staff must purchase for themselves.

> **Try This: On-Demand Onboarding**
>
> Leverage technology to provide on-demand onboarding. Create a hyper-doc—a Microsoft Word or Google Docs document with active links to directions, images, or videos that explain various school expectations and events. Use tools such as Screencastify or Loom to record procedures to help newcomers visualize components of school operations. Use tools such as Canva, Kami, or Google Drawings to create maps and charts to clarify processes for using spaces around the building. Here are some specific examples of things to include in your on-demand onboarding:
>
> - Bus arrival and dismissal procedures
> - Car rider arrival and dismissal procedures
> - Breakfast and lunch procedures
> - Faculty sign-in/sign-out
> - Attendance and tardiness documentation
> - Discipline guidelines and referrals
> - Field trip approval and forms
> - Bookkeeping
> - Staff absences
> - Food delivery
> - Policy regarding leaving school during the workday
> - Other handbook items
>
> One school that Jessica served at had an "All the Links" document where school leaders provided just what the title suggests: links to frequently needed documents. Offering this kind of easy access can help new teachers—and all teachers, in fact—manage the abundance of information.

## Organizing an Orientation Session

Many of the elements of the onboarding process we've described can be covered in a well-organized orientation session. If new hires are unable to attend such a session, provide them with short video clips of procedures and locations (these can also be shared with anyone who may need a reminder).

When Jessica served as the lead mentor for a middle school, she offered a half-day orientation for new staff. The main focus was meeting the support staff and learning whom to go to for what, and where to find necessary resources. She was intentional in including non-teaching staff in these conversations because, as noted before, they play crucial roles in school operations. New staff were able to meet people such as the custodian, nurse, secretary, bookkeeper, school resource officer/security, and administrators.

In addition, a one-page handout detailing who does what and where to find them was distributed, along with a calendar of school holidays, spring break, and faculty meetings—information that's important to all staff but that can help new hires in particular get organized and plan ahead. The calendar also listed contact information for district office support personnel and elected representatives who served the school community. Teachers also left the orientation with their copy code and knowledge of how to use the copier, as well as how to make sure their email was working, get keys to classrooms, and use the poster maker and laminator. They learned about sign-in procedures for faculty, car line procedures, duty areas and expectations, the location of the fridge and microwave for lunchtime use, discipline-related procedures, student hall pass procedures, and other operations-related items that are often understood by existing staff but can take time to learn.

Every school has unique procedures that need to be communicated to new staff. Mastering these seemingly small matters can influence how successful a new teacher feels in the first few weeks of school. Proactively addressing them prevents frustration and enables your new colleagues to focus on effective instruction.

## Mentoring and Layers of Support

It's important to connect new staff with a mentor who will be responsible for communicating and providing guidance during the onboarding process. Be strategic in pairing new hires with mentors; avoid staff who are cliquish. Make sure the mentor clearly understands the responsibilities of the role and the need to proactively support their mentee. Provide training and preparation time to equip mentors to facilitate the best possible onboarding experience for new staff. Don't assume mentors are meeting the expectations of the mentoring role without verifying by checking in with both mentor and mentee to assess the effectiveness of the pairing. Sometimes one partner fails to put forth effort to be an active participant. Checking in with each person separately can help determine the cause of the reluctance or disengagement.

If you have many new hires, keep the mentor–mentee ratio at no more than one to three. It's difficult to maintain enriching relationships with numerous mentees. Although new staff will benefit from relationships with multiple colleagues, assign one person specifically to them to help with the onboarding process. Be sure this person is someone other than a team leader or department chair. The onboarding mentor should focus on welcoming, onboarding, and creating a sense of belonging for the new hire, proactively connecting with their mentee to create a safe space for reflection, processing, and growth. The mentor can also help direct the new staff member toward resources and other support layers as needed.

That said, newly hired teachers do need multiple layers of support from different staff members. Consider differing backgrounds when establishing layers of support. Mentors with distinct perspectives create a dynamic support structure. The second-year teacher may offer recent, relatable advice, whereas the veteran mentor can provide historical context and share strategies that have withstood the test of time. Diversity will ensure that the new teacher receives a comprehensive understanding of the teaching profession and the school, encompassing both contemporary and time-tested approaches.

When Carrie had a student teacher who subsequently joined her school's faculty, she ended up serving as all of his layers of support. She was his team lead, department chair, collaborative partner, and mentor. In retrospect, it would have been better for him to draw on the experiences of several people rather than just one.

A benefit of layered support is that it gives teachers more opportunities to make authentic connections with staff. Content-based assistance, such as that offered by a department chair, district coach, or collaborative teaching partner, can provide targeted support to help new teachers improve their instructional practices and content knowledge. This can be especially valuable for those who are new to teaching a particular subject or content area. Grade-level support can help the teacher to navigate the unique challenges and opportunities of teaching that particular grade or as part of that particular team. The support can include guidance on procedures, classroom management, and working with parents and students. The person providing the support is often a team or grade-level teacher-leader who can answer questions related to grade level–specific items. If existing structures for either type of support are already in place, you may not need to formally establish them.

With over 20 years of school leadership experience, retired principal Norma Faerber has given a lot of thought to how to best facilitate mentoring relationships for new teachers. She emphasizes the role of strategic support:

> Providing grade-level or content-specific teams that meet regularly for planning and sharing ideas is a must in onboarding new hires. Providing at least two mentors who are complementary to the new hire in terms of interests or personality and who are not on the same grade level or content team adds to that new hire's available resources within the school. A first-year teacher can benefit from the support of a second-year teacher who just finished walking the first-year walk, but that new teacher can also benefit from the support of a veteran teacher who has been in the profession for several years and possesses a wealth of experience and knowledge about students, parents, and the life of schools. So two mentors with different perspectives are important for support. Asking each member to share some of the ways they manage to use the mentorship relationship can be helpful to everyone. The relationships require commitment, accountability, and consistency. They cannot be in name only.

Years ago, as a new teacher, Carrie greatly benefited from her experience with being mentored. Almost every afternoon, one or two teachers would stop by Carrie's classroom to talk with her and ask thoughtful questions that allowed her to reflect on her teaching practice that day. After listening and not judging, these veteran teachers would ask additional questions, listen, offer suggestions and strategies, and express encouragement. On days when Carrie was filled with self-doubt, her mentors always seemed to have the words she needed to hear. Two years later, Carrie was selected Teacher of the Year—not just for the school but for the entire district. Those early years were filled with growth for students and for Carrie, and more than 25 years later, the simple practices followed by her mentors still prove effective in welcoming new teachers and equipping them to be contributing members of the team.

## Monitoring Mentorship

Give each mentor and mentee a handout with dates for monthly meetings throughout the year. Schedule these regular check-ins to ensure the right support is being provided at the right time. For example, at the appropriate times, the mentor can offer guidance on testing protocols, expectations regarding parent communication, welcome letters to students at the start of the year, gradebook setup, and teacher observations. Think about the school year and design a monthly checklist based on what a new teacher in your building will need to know and be able to do to be successful. See Figure 3.4 for an example of a midyear checklist for a mentoring meeting.

FIGURE 3.4

**Sample Checklist for Mentoring Meeting**

| December Mentoring Checklist ||
|---|---|
| **Completed** | **Topics** |
| | Inclement weather procedures (e.g., two-hour delay or early dismissal, communicating with parents, student transportation changes, adapting instruction for shorter days) |
| | Finalizing grades for first semester |
| | Class parties, holiday concerts, staff holiday events |
| | [Open space for mentee questions] |

## Beyond the Checklist

Of course, an onboarding mentor can go beyond the formal mentoring checklist. Doing so can create a sense of community and collaboration, help to build a culture of continuous improvement, and provide teachers with a support system that can help them navigate the challenges of teaching. Welcoming support can come in many forms. Here are some examples of what onboarding mentors can do:

- Invite the mentee to sit with them in group settings.
- Invite the mentee to join them for lunch.
- Engage in authentic conversations about the school, the role, and the community.
- Initiate informal check-ins ("How are things going overall, not just in the classroom and the school?").
- Provide words of encouragement and affirmation.
- Show up in the mentee's room and say, "I'm here. How can I help?"
- Speak to the mentee in hallways and other school settings outside the classroom.

During Carrie's first year of teaching in 1995, she taught 1st grade. She was assigned a mentor who would frequently stop by at the end of the school day and ask how the day had gone. These conversations with a trusted mentor encouraged Carrie to problem-solve and refine her practice under the guidance of a veteran teacher. There was not anything planned or complicated about these check-ins, but they benefited students and helped Carrie grow during a critical time in her career.

## M-n-M Meetings

Structured ways for multiple mentor–mentee dyads to come together help expand support beyond checking off items on the checklist; we like to call them M-n-M (mentor-and-mentee) meetings. The collective wisdom expressed in such meetings can benefit all participants. It's important to design M-n-M meetings to include equity of voice and collaborative tasks. We recommend they be facilitated by a school leader who is not serving as a mentor to allow for a balance of power between mentors and mentees, which creates an inclusive environment and invites candid conversations. Leaders can decide the frequency of meetings (e.g., monthly, bimonthly, quarterly). Mentors and mentees should sit side by side to converse and complete tasks as equals. This seems obvious; however, Carrie once walked into an M-n-M meeting where all the mentors sat together, leaving all the mentees to sit in their own group. This setup—whether intentional or unintentional—conveyed a sense of higher status for mentors, an environment that did not feel psychologically safe for mentees. As such, it was a missed opportunity for growth for both groups.

Establishing structures and expectations for M-n-M meetings creates conditions for inclusion, respect, and growth. One goal of such meetings might be to facilitate the development of clear guidelines for mentoring partnerships. For instance, the group might determine a protocol for how and when feedback will be given after classroom observations (immediate or at a later time) and what format it should take (written or oral). Setting these guidelines upfront as a group can create a foundation of trust and clarity, ensuring that the mentoring partnerships in the school are productive and mutually beneficial. It's also important to design M-n-M meetings in response to data such as feedback from mentors and mentees, and observations (both formal and informal).

The agendas for M-n-M meetings should include activities that both build relationships and address the needs of both mentees and mentors. Here are some suggestions:

- Wellness practices
  - Stress-reducing strategies such as breathing exercises
  - Mindset work such as Circle of Influence versus Circle of Concern, a concept that distinguishes between things that you can actually influence or control and things that are matters of concern but beyond your control
  - Humor such as Kid President videos (e.g., *A Pep Talk from Kid President to You,* found on YouTube [Participant, 2013])

- Noticing and naming emotions
  - "First Month Feels," during which participants share feelings of success and feelings of frustration during the incredibly challenging first few months of teaching
  - An emoji chart or emotions wheel to communicate feelings beyond the first month to uncover teachers' unmet needs and take appropriate actions
- Book study
  - Books with topics that align with school goals, support educator growth, or address student needs
  - Creative tasks to share learning from book studies, such as using memes or songs to describe a chapter
- Team-building tasks
  - Shared experiences to build connections among staff
  - Challenges to leverage collaborative problem solving
- Deprivatizing practice
  - Shared problems of practice, using a protocol for discussion
  - Feedback on planned lesson, task, or assessment

Don't overlook the importance of helping new staff feel successful by addressing two critical issues: classroom management and behavior expectations. One of the challenges of classroom management is anticipating and being prepared to respond to situations never before experienced. Consider providing time for teachers who are new to your building—and who may or may not be new to teaching—to discuss with their mentor how they might respond to a particular situation and role-play their solution. We encourage you to practice with the kinds of challenges that are most common in your building, which may include the following:

- Students talking across the classroom during what should be quiet learning or practice time
- Students taking too long to settle in and get to work after they enter the classroom
- Students frequently entering the classroom late

Effective mentoring requires intentional planning, integrity in implementation, and commitment to reflection and refinement. Although as a school leader you may not be serving as a mentor, you're the person creating the time and space for mentoring to occur. If possible, pay stipends for serving as a mentor or participating in M-n-M meetings. If stipends are not an option, consider offering a reduction in other duties, such as monitoring the cafeteria or the parking lot. Remember to periodically evaluate whether the M-n-M meetings are being implemented and yielding the desired outcomes.

---

**Try This: A Leader's Schedule of Support for Onboarding**

Ultimately, the goal of onboarding new teachers is to create a welcoming and supportive environment that facilitates a smooth transition and integration into the school community. By establishing clear expectations, providing ongoing support and guidance, and fostering a culture of inclusion and collaboration, schools can help new staff invest in the organization and feel valued for their contributions. Use the task list below to keep track of your performance in this important area of school leadership.

**Summer**

- Have you prepared for onboarding new hires?
  - Have rooms been cleaned?
  - Have technology and instructional resources been gathered?
- Have you scheduled welcoming opportunities such as a school tour, a tour of the school community, and classroom setup time?
- Have you prepared educators to serve as mentors?
- Have you connected mentors and mentees?

**Back to School (August/September)**

- Have you informed new hires about when to report to work?
- Have you put structures and expectations in place for regular mentoring?

**First Semester**

- How do you know that mentors are having conversations with their mentees?
- How are you soliciting feedback and checking in on new staff?
- What changes or adjustments will you make to ensure better outcomes in the second semester?

**Second Semester**

- How are you maintaining momentum with the mentorship model?
- How are you soliciting feedback and checking in on new staff?
- How are you communicating plans for next year, including staffing?

> **End of School (May/June)**
> - How are you celebrating the mentoring program? Have you provided certificates of completion?
> - How are you providing time to reflect and set goals?
>   - Are you soliciting feedback on the effectiveness of the mentoring program?
>   - Are you conducting exit interviews with staff who are leaving?
>   - Are you conducting stay interviews with staff who are staying?
> - How are you sharing information about summer professional development opportunities?
> - How are you communicating room changes or role changes?
> - How are you informing staff about when the building will be open during summer months?
> - How are you informing staff as to when other groups will be using the building, including classrooms, for events during the summer?

## Creating a Team Culture for Welcoming and Onboarding

Welcoming and onboarding processes and activities can be critical in helping teachers develop their skills and expertise and in establishing a supportive and collaborative school culture. One teacher shared the following about her experience as a new hire:

> I was invited to a training over the summer—and paid a stipend to attend—to learn about my new district. Representatives from every sector of the district presented on a wide range of topics. There were follow-up meetings and check-ins to make sure we were settling in. There was also swag to brand us as part of the team. I felt supported, seen, and heard.

This teacher greatly valued her onboarding experience, which her school leaders had clearly put a lot of thought into. Although someone else may lead the effort and mentors may be more directly involved, ultimately you set the expectations for the treatment of new staff members in your school.

It's important to share information about newcomers with existing staff members and encourage a warm and welcoming environment. This can include suggesting that current staff members invite new staff to sit with them at school events, such as football games, or eat lunch with them on inservice training days. Schools can be very cliquish. From the new hire's perspective, it doesn't feel good when everyone else has plans and they're not included. Discourage displays of status among current staff members.

Socialization—integrating newcomers into the school community and ensuring that they feel a sense of belonging and connection—sets the tone for how staff will act and interact. Don't assume it will happen without defining expectations and providing a framework, such as by planning organized social activities that take place during paid work time in a location accessible to everyone. Be sure to take into account the preferences of your staff. Although an offsite location may provide fun activities to build community, it may not suit the accessibility and comfort level requirements for all. An outdoor get-together when it's 100 degrees is not a comfortable setting, and outdoor locations may not be accessible for wheelchair users or people with mobility restrictions. Additionally, avoid providing alcoholic beverages at planned social events for at least three reasons: (1) the district's professional code of conduct probably forbids alcohol consumption at school-sponsored events, (2) it could result in poor decision making and negative interactions, and (3) it can isolate individuals who do not partake for religious or other reasons or are dealing with or recovering from addiction. Plan socialization events in a safe environment that provides opportunities for shared experiences and positive interactions.

Planned socialization shouldn't stop after the first month of school. Events should be scheduled throughout the year to promote staff bonding and shared experiences. Include socialization experiences on staff inservice training days and at meetings throughout the year. Frequent, embedded team-building opportunities create staff-to-staff connections that will increase a sense of belonging.

> **Try This: Socializing Through Structured Shared Experiences**
>
> Organized activities such as the ones described below can provide a focus for socialization and can be a fun way to integrate newcomers into the school community.

### Meet My Colleague

For the first round, use numbers or symbols to organize staff into pairs. Each person listens to their partner introduce themselves, using index cards to take notes on key details so they can introduce them in the next round. In the second round, each pair joins another pair, and each person introduces their original partner. This second round serves as a practice session. For the third round, staff take 60 to 90 seconds to introduce their first-round colleague to the whole group. Introduce the American Sign Language (ASL) sign for "me too" (make the sign for "Y" and slide your hand back and forth between you and the speaker), and have group members use the sign to indicate a connection with details shared about the person being introduced. This activity takes time, but building a team where everyone feels welcome and valued is worth the investment.

### This or That

Have a list or slide deck of conversation starters featuring brief questions with two answer options—for example, "Dessert: pie or cake?" Either in partners or small groups, have staff members pick an option and share their reason. Low-risk topics can provide a starting point for conversations that lead colleagues to learn more about one another.

### Lego Blind Build

This activity is a shared experience that leverages interdependent teamwork. Working in groups of five, staff members assemble a Lego kit (using the same kit for each group builds a sense of competition around which group will complete the task first). Each group member has a defined role. Builder A and Builder B can only manipulate the Lego bricks. Communicator A can only talk to the team members. Communicator B can take notes and sketch, as well as talk to team members. The Communicators are also the only ones allowed to see a completed kit, hidden from view nearby. The Directions Interpreter accesses the Lego instruction pages, which have been torn apart and laid out at random, and relays information verbally to the team. Teams with fewer than five members can select which role to eliminate. This activity usually takes 45 to 60 minutes to complete.

### Pieces of the Puzzle

In this activity, each staff member gets a fraction of the pieces that make up a larger puzzle, symbolizing how each member contributes to the bigger picture at school. As participants work on the puzzle together, they can take time to chat, share thoughts, and get to know the unique skills that each team member brings to the table. The puzzle is a metaphor for the collective efforts to create a positive learning environment for all students.

## Building a Culture of Inclusivity

A culture of inclusivity is integral to welcoming new hires, and building such a culture requires intentional efforts. Don't assume everyone will support and welcome new hires. Sometimes veteran teachers can be territorial and exclude newcomers because they feel threatened. Take action to promote and value collaboration over competition. Ask yourself, "What barriers need to be removed? How can I be sure new hires feel enabled and empowered?"

## Cultural and Other Differences

Use the acronym INCLUDE to identify strategies for welcoming educators to your school who may differ in some way from you or the majority of your current faculty.

- *I*nstill inclusive language practices
- *N*urture cultural competency through training
- *C*learly communicate values related to inclusivity
- *L*ink educators through affinity groups
- *U*se anonymous feedback channels to gather honest information about concerns, reactions (both positive and negative), and potential issues
- *D*elve into considerations regarding accessibility
- *E*ncourage mutual support and guidance

It's important to be mindful that new—and current—staff members may not hold the same personal beliefs or customs you do. For example, dietary restrictions due to religious beliefs or medical conditions should be considered when providing food for staff. Use the INCLUDE acronym as a tool for reflection when designing adult learning and staff development experiences.

## Generational Acceptance

Generational differences refer to the distinct characteristics, values, behaviors, and attitudes associated with individuals from different birth cohorts, or generations. These differences are shaped by the social, economic, and cultural events that occur during a particular time period. Although it's important to note that not everyone within a generation will share the same traits, tendencies, or perspectives, observable patterns often emerge. Here are some of the general characteristics associated with the various generations (McCrindle, n.d.):

- Baby Boomers (born 1946–1964)
  - Post–World War II generation
  - Often associated with values such as loyalty to the organization, work ethic, and hierarchical authority
  - May prefer more traditional communication methods such as phone calls rather than texting
- Generation X (born 1965–1980)
  - Experienced economic and social changes such as the rise of dual-income households
  - Often characterized by independence, adaptability, and a preference for a flatter hierarchy
  - Adapted to technology advancements as they occurred
- Millennials, or Generation Y (born 1981–1996)
  - Grew up during the rise of the internet and rapid technological advancements
  - Value work-life balance, diversity, and social responsibility
  - Tend to be tech-savvy, collaborative, and seek purpose in their work
- Generation Z (born 1997–2010)
  - The first generation to grow up with easy access to technology and the internet from a young age
  - Value inclusivity, diversity, and authenticity
  - More likely to be entrepreneurial and globally aware
- Generation Alpha (born 2010–2024)
  - Experienced the effects of the COVID-19 pandemic in their youth and the shift to online learning and digital tools such as AI
  - Value innovation, entrepreneurship, and sustainability
  - More likely to be environmentally aware and pursue nontraditional career paths

Each generation brings unique perspectives, communication styles, and expectations to the workplace. Recognizing and understanding these generational differences can promote effective communication, teamwork, and employee engagement. It's essential for organizations to create a workplace culture that values diversity and inclusivity, allowing for the strengths of each generation to contribute to overall success. However, it's also important to avoid broad generalizations or stereotypes based on generational differences. Individuals are influenced by a complex interplay of factors, and considerable diversity is evident within each generation.

In the ever-evolving education landscape, acknowledging and embracing generational differences is key to creating a collaborative and enriching environment for both new and seasoned educators. One effective way to promote generational acceptance is through structuring the kind of strategic mentorship program and layers of support described earlier in this chapter. Generational acceptance and mentorship are integral components of a thriving school community. By fostering connections between educators of different generations, school leaders can create a supportive ecosystem where knowledge, experience, and innovation can be seamlessly passed down, benefiting educators and, most important, the students they serve.

## Integrating New Hires into the Community

Invite new staff to be involved in opportunities that extend beyond their classroom teaching responsibilities. Don't assume that they lack skills or expertise because they're new. Make a list of all of the opportunities at the school, from extracurricular activities and events to helping colleagues with day-to-day tasks that may require a specific skill set. Ask new hires to mark their top three interests. Self-reporting their interest and expertise will help you identify pathways of involvement and growth for them.

One example of getting new teachers involved in extended activities is the apprentice approach. Every teacher leader can benefit from having an apprentice. For example, the teacher in charge of the yearbook needs an apprentice so that more than one person holds the knowledge and expertise necessary for the yearbook to exist. An apprenticeship structure helps to ensure that new hires are fully contributing members of the school team.

> **Try This: Conduct a Strengths Showcase**
>
> A strengths showcase helps new staff identify their strengths, talents, and areas of expertise, providing opportunities for them to apply these skills in their new role. Each teacher is asked to think of three strengths and write them on a chart, along with a brief description of how they envision using them in the school setting. Next, teachers do a gallery walk and respond on signed sticky notes to at least 10 colleagues with opportunities to connect and collaborate around future efforts to do meaningful work for students and the school. For example, a teacher who enjoys and has skill in using Canva for graphic design might say they hope to use this strength to create communications for school events. Knowing this, someone can ask them for help as needs arise, such as a request to design T-shirts for the school chorus.
>
> A strengths showcase can help new staff feel valued and appreciated for their unique contributions. Those feelings, in turn, can lead to increased job satisfaction and commitment—an outcome that makes this activity potentially beneficial to a wider audience. Consider implementing such a showcase not just for new teachers but for all staff.

## The Lasting Effects of Welcoming and Onboarding

Welcoming new employees is crucial for several reasons, as it sets the tone for their entire experience within the organization. First impressions matter. The initial interactions with a new employee are lasting. A warm welcome demonstrates that the organization values its employees and is committed to creating a positive work environment. It helps the new person feel included and part of the team from the start. This sense of belonging is crucial for building strong interpersonal connections and encouraging collaboration. Starting a new job can be stressful, and new hires may feel anxious about fitting in and understanding their roles. A welcoming environment helps alleviate these concerns, allowing the employee to focus on their responsibilities.

A well-structured onboarding process helps new employees quickly understand the school's culture, values, and expectations, which accelerates their integration into the organization and ensures they can contribute effectively to their team. Employees who have a positive onboarding experience are more likely to be engaged, motivated, and committed to their roles.

As you develop your welcoming and onboarding processes, celebrate what's working. Provide positive feedback to staff around welcoming efforts that result in the desired onboarding experience, but also take time to reflect and refine your efforts, making necessary changes. Don't assume you have to wait until next year to revise your approaches. Address the deficits, adjust, and respond quickly.

## Empathy Episode

Read the following Empathy Episode and imagine what it would feel like to be in the teacher's position. Then use the reflection questions to consider leadership blind spots and how to remedy them.

> Reflecting on your first year teaching at a school with low turnover and high community involvement, you realize that your school-based mentor never checked in with you or offered to help you. Neither did the department chair or team leader. Even though your mentor is a longtime teacher at the school and someone who is good-natured, she tends to keep to herself and not take initiative. You often felt like you were bothering her when you asked questions or sought feedback. She never invited you to lunch during professional development days. You wonder why she was chosen to be a mentor.
>
> Although you had support from the district throughout the year, your school had no structures to support you. You felt isolated and disconnected. Additionally, the principal publicly stated that you were the strongest teacher in your content area, which had the unintended consequence of perceived competition and disconnect from the other teachers in that area. Your grade-level team leader asked you, "Are you trying to take my job?" Another colleague said, "You're making us all look bad." These remarks not only were hurtful but also made you want to isolate and protect yourself. Furthermore, you began to wonder if you needed to compromise your teaching practices in order to "belong" at this school. You made a genuine connection with only one teacher, and when that person chose to leave to teach at another school in the district, you began to consider other schools as options as well.

### Reflection Questions

- How could the teacher's experience of the first year at a new school be improved?
- What can school leaders do to ensure structures are in place that welcome staff and create a sense of belonging?

This scenario illustrates the failure of the school leader to monitor the new hire's experience in receiving support, which could have occurred during feedback sessions after classroom observations or in a brief one-on-one check-in with the teacher. Establishing a schedule for mentor check-ins can provide both accountability and assistance to the mentors. A school leader meeting with the mentors could have revealed the lack of follow-through in the mentoring program. Similarly, checking in with department or team leads regarding support for the new hire could have revealed a disconnect.

Although the school leader in this case had good intentions when recognizing the new hire's efforts, publicly praising the newcomer in this way created resentment among staff. It also helped perpetuate a culture of status and competition rather than collaboration; the school leader was "ranking" teachers rather than promoting collective efficacy and impact. The leader could instead have acknowledged the new hire's quality of instruction during feedback sessions and asked how the layers of support at the school were contributing to that, thus providing an opportunity for the new hire to discuss the actual situation—namely, the lack of mentoring and support from the staff. Moreover, in a change of approach, the leader could have used a faculty or department meeting to celebrate each person's successes and identify areas for support. Normalizing support for both new and veteran staff would create a safe environment for growth, which would improve the school's culture.

More generally, the scenario illustrates the importance of addressing Maslow's hierarchy of needs—specifically, those concerned with physiology, safety, love and belonging, and esteem. Consider how your school and you as its leader are meeting these needs. Be sure new hires know where to store their belongings, where to store and prepare food they may bring from home, and which restroom to use. Provide clear information about all safety drills and protocols for arrival and dismissal. This kind of knowledge may seem mundane, but it helps newcomers feel safe and relaxed enough to do their best work. Acknowledge that the individual's talent is being used to further the school's mission and vision. Create a welcoming culture and celebrate the person's unique contributions to the team and the larger school community.

## How Will You Commit?

- What strategies from this chapter are you committed to implementing?
- Who can help you implement these strategies?
- What outcome do you want to see as a result of implementing these strategies?

## Summary

In this chapter, we discussed how to welcome new staff to your school, including providing multiple layers of support so that more than one person provides a welcoming environment. Onboarding and providing mentoring support for new hires can be the gateway to making sure they know their professional fulfillment is a priority, which is the focus of Chapter 4.

# 4

# Prioritizing People

*After spending many years as a school/district administrator, I chose to spend a year as an elementary math coach and consultant in a school district. Two months into the position, the superintendent reached out to meet. I assumed this would be about what I was able to accomplish in the position to date and next steps, but instead he was just checking in to see how it was going. Despite the fact that this was not an administrative position, it was really nice to have a lengthy conversation about both the role and educational leadership in general. We spoke for quite a while, and I felt valued as a leader and employee when he gave his incredibly valuable time so willingly. The feelings of value and empowerment continued to motivate me as I moved forward to do the most I could to serve the teachers and students throughout the district.*

—Kathryn Lemerich, STEM supervisor

The biggest investment a school district makes is the human capital that implements each school's vision and mission. As a school leader, prioritizing the people in your care is essential. How do you do this in a way that meets your staff's need for love, belonging, and esteem?

We make time for what we value. Do you make time for your staff? Do you acknowledge their strengths and accomplishments?

Distractions can easily become excuses. Necessary but nonpriority tasks—"I just need to check my email" or "I need to fill out this form"—become a never-ending list of action items that draw leaders away from the people in the building. Given the demands of the job, there will always be a list of action items. What might not always be there are great educators, people who give their time and talents to the job. Reciprocate their investment by prioritizing them. Ask yourself often, "What really matters?"

In this chapter, we'll explore how to prioritize people by being present and showing your appreciation as a leader. Before continuing, take a moment to consider your current situation in this area by completing the self-assessment in Figure 4.1.

FIGURE 4.1

**Prioritizing People Self-Assessment**

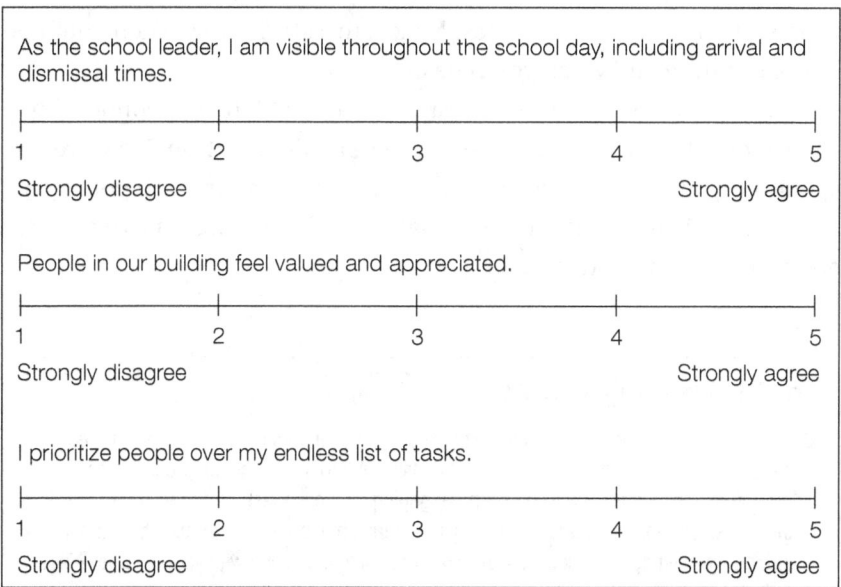

## The Power of Physical Presence

Being physically present communicates to staff that availability is a priority for you. It's disheartening for a teacher to need support and not know where their administrator is. It's infuriating to need support and know their administrator is deskbound. There's power in being physically present around the building. Visibility conveys "I am here with you" and communicates a mutual agreement that both parties take responsibility for the work. Being present among the staff also provides opportunities to invite conversations. A teacher shared with Carrie and Jessica how a principal intentionally scheduled time to visit every classroom at least once a week to see learning in action. This time spent in classrooms opened doors to conversations with faculty.

When considering how to make yourself available, keep in mind teachers' planning and lunch times. If you eat lunch or have a meeting at the same time each day, you may be inadvertently reducing your accessibility to teachers who have planning periods or lunch during those times. Be aware of how your schedule might conflict with others' schedules. Consider how to make yours more flexible to avoid consistent and recurring issues. Make sure staff know when you'll be in the building and when you'll be out.

Time will always be a constraining factor. Consider conducting a time audit like the one described in the Try This section. How are you spending your time? Does your time allotment align with your goals and values? Make every moment matter by dedicating time to be present with teachers and students.

> **Try This: Conduct a Time Audit**
>
> Create a table with three or four columns labeled with your various work responsibilities and a column labeled "Other" for work that doesn't fit into any of the other categories. For a week, record how much time you spend engaging with each task category. At the end of the week, tally your time and create a visual representation, such as a pie chart, a bar graph, or a percentage list. Reflect. Does your time allotment align with your priorities? This exercise may affirm that your time is spent in accordance with your goals, or it may help you discover obstacles that are getting in the way of how you spend your time.

Be in classrooms as much as possible, especially when invited. When educators get excited about a lesson or student work, they want to share that feeling with others. We make time for what we value, so make time to be present in learning experiences with teachers and students. Teachers spend hours preparing and teaching. Reciprocate the investment by visiting classrooms with the sole purpose of witnessing learning in action. As a coach, if Carrie found she had some open time in her schedule, she would visit classrooms, sometimes leaving a positive message on a sticky note. These spontaneous visits often led to follow-up conversations with teachers about student learning or next steps in planning. Yes, formal observations are necessary, but they should take up a small portion of the time you spend in the presence of teaching and learning.

Outside the classroom, attending professional development sessions alongside teachers is another way to be present. Active participation shows that you value professional growth for yourself and your staff. It also equips you with the knowledge to provide meaningful feedback on matters related to the sessions.

Keep in mind that teachers and students may not seek you out. You won't realize what you're missing if you stay in your office answering emails. Think about where you locate yourself during the day and the message your location sends about your priorities. One morning, when Jessica was monitoring the hallway as students transitioned to their next class, a teacher approached and asked her to come by to observe a science lab lesson. Jessica found 20 minutes in her schedule to visit the class, which led to an invitation to the teacher's planning session to look at student work. Being in the right spot at the right time led to a positive coaching opportunity. You can't make that happen if you're not intentionally making yourself available and only engage in predictable, repeated interactions.

Your physical presence also provides an opportunity to bond over shared experiences, engage in informal conversation, and develop closer relationships. For example, during a planning session, Jessica was talking about rearranging the classroom to promote student discourse and used the term "squircle," combining the words *square* and *circle*. The conversation may have been trivial and the invented word silly, but the experience bonded those who were present, and they often used the word in future conversations. It was a reminder of that moment and reaffirmed a positive view of each other. Shared experiences like this one create a sense of closeness and connection and build rapport with staff.

Being physically present invites informal conversation. Staff cannot speak to you if you're never around. Small talk can reveal big issues, which can help you, as a leader, to proactively address emerging challenges. Casual conversation, free from status or an agenda, builds trust and comradery, leading teachers and staff to feel heard and valued. Never miss an opportunity to listen. The concept of *propinquity* manifests when exposure is paired with frequency, resulting in a closer relationship between two individuals. In other words, proximity matters. When leaders are physically near their staff, the likelihood of conversation and shared experiences increases and relationships with staff improve.

Here are some tips for prioritizing people with your physical presence throughout the day:

- Set a reminder to be in the hallways during class changes.
- Post a weekly schedule somewhere visible, including times when you'll be off campus.
- Have lunch with grade-level or content-area teams (if scheduling permits).
- Keep track of formal and informal class visits to ensure equitable investment of your time.
- Schedule time during teacher planning to be available to meet with staff.
- Develop a routine for greeting staff as they arrive at school.
- Establish a role in the dismissal process.

Be a leader on the move! One way to accomplish this is to use a mobile cart for a satellite desk. A rolling cart large enough to hold a laptop device provides a way to be near teachers and students while also responding to emails and handling other routine tasks. This visibility removes the mystery of what a school leader does all day. If you opt to work solely from your office desk, one way to be on the move is to "take a lap" after each task is completed. Let's be honest. Being a school leader involves enough desk work to take up the entire day, but it's important to move throughout the building to get a sense of the climate of the school. Being more visible in different areas can strengthen the sense of community and connection between you and your staff.

## Classrooms First, Checklists Second

In her coaching experience, Carrie has heard teachers express disappointment when school or district leaders have repeatedly turned down or ignored invitations to visit classrooms citing a lack of time. One teacher invited the school principal and assistant principal several times to come and see students' culminating presentations, and not once during the year were they able to make it. Over time, this led to the teacher feeling hurt and devalued, and the work felt less worthy of time from both the teacher and administration.

## The Four Ss of Showing Up

The essence of being present can be expressed in the simple statement "Just show up." In a scene in the movie *The Break-Up* (Reed, 2006), a couple argues in the kitchen about doing the dishes. Jennifer Aniston's character says, "I want you to *want* to do the dishes," and Vince Vaughn's character replies, "Why would I want to do the dishes?" This exchange illustrates the frustration of obligation versus self-motivation. We feel gratitude when someone shows up without being pressured by an invitation or a sense of obligation. Educators want to be supported in this way, especially by leadership.

Siegel and Bryson (2020) identify what they call the Four *S*s of showing up—*safe, seen, soothed, secure*—in their discussion about how children develop secure attachments with their caregivers, and they emphasize the notion of being not perfect but present. The same ideas can be applied to school leadership, as shown in Figure 4.2. A flawed leader is preferable to an absent one.

In her role as a district innovation coach, Jessica had an experience that illustrates the power of just showing up. One morning, with an hour of unscheduled time before a school meeting, she stopped by another school she was supporting to check in on an educator launching a new program. As Jessica walked into the classroom, the teacher met her with a quizzical look. Jessica responded, "We don't have a meeting this morning, but I wanted to check in with you before heading to another meeting." Hearing this, the teacher began to cry. Her implementation of the new program wasn't going well, and she'd been trying to figure out why. As the teacher described the steps, Jessica realized one crucial element was missing and shared her observation. Problem solved. In a matter of minutes, she had soothed this educator's anxiety and frustration, leading the teacher to feel secure in her ability to teach the lesson. Because this interaction occurred early in the school year, the coach-teacher partnership was strengthened. It also established an understanding that support for innovation would be ongoing and that Jessica would make time to "just show up."

FIGURE 4.2

## A School Leader's Version of the Four Ss of Showing Up

Staff feel *safe* when you respond with support, not judgment, whenever they try a new approach or take a risk. Entering a classroom with a clipboard or a laptop can inadvertently convey judgment. Instead, leaving a positive message on a sticky note on your way out is a great way to convey your support. Encouraging staff to take risks, acknowledging mistakes as part of the learning process, and welcoming diversity of thought create an environment where educators feel psychologically safe to learn and grow.

Staff feel *seen* when you acknowledge and speak to them whenever you encounter them in the building or in other settings. Doing so also allows you to be responsive to their emotional well-being and stay attuned to the climate of the school.

Staff feel *soothed* when you are present to help calm them through times of stress or disruption. Providing direction and reassurance during difficult times is an opportunity to ease anxiety and be a source of comfort. In addition, leading alongside your staff communicates a collective approach to navigating issues and obstacles, which can be reassuring in itself.

Staff feel *secure* when you empower them to make decisions, affirming their value as a faculty member. More broadly, a sense of security relates directly to the other three Ss. Making teachers and staff feel *safe, seen,* and *soothed* leads them to be *secure* in their ability to do their best work, to be reassured of their professional worth, and to persevere through challenging situations.

We all want to feel connected and valued. Leaders reveal what they value by what they make time for and participate in. Create time and space to connect with faculty and share experiences with them. Invest your minutes to make memorable moments with the people who matter most.

## Tuning In with Mental Presence and Emotional Awareness

A high school marketing teacher shared a time when an administrator scheduled a meeting to discuss an idea for a field trip the teacher had proposed during a faculty meeting. The teacher was hopeful that the field trip would be approved, especially because students at the school had limited experiences beyond their neighborhood. The trip would have provided work-based learning opportunities at various companies around the area and a tour of the local community college. As the teacher entered the office, the administrator was finishing a call but waved the teacher to come in. Then the administrator started typing but asked the teacher to share the details of the proposed field trip. The teacher began speaking with enthusiasm that tapered off as she realized that the administrator had not stopped typing or made eye contact. The teacher slowed down but continued to talk and ended with a question. The administrator's silence indicated a failure to realize that a question had been asked or the talking had stopped. So the teacher waited a few moments before repeating the question a bit louder, which got a response. The administrator looked up and said, "Sounds good. Fill out the forms." The teacher later shared that the joy of getting approval was overshadowed by the administration's disinterest.

Have you ever been talking and realized that the other person is not paying attention? Active listening tells the other person that we value what they have to say. At the same time, the more comfortable leaders are with staff, the more comfortable they can feel about multitasking. If you're in the midst of dealing with a time-sensitive issue and can't give a staff member your full attention, ask the person to pause while you complete the task. Explain that what they have to say is important and deserves your attention, and that's why you've asked them to pause. Pausing ensures that staff are heard and that you can respectfully respond. One-word responses do not convey value.

Another way leaders can be more attuned to what another person is saying is by asking how that person wants you to respond. Jessica started using the SOS (Solutions or Sighs) method during meetings with new teachers to allow the teachers to share but also give them control in how others respond. This method allows the person describing an issue to choose whether they want the listener to either generate possible solutions or be an empathetic listener who sighs with the speaker as a sign of understanding. Sometimes the speaker will ask for both, in which case the speaker and the listener sigh together and then talk through possible solutions.

## Focusing on What Matters

Mental presence improves as we focus. But how can leaders focus when there are so many needs and demands vying for attention? If someone you encounter in a hallway wants to have an on-the-spot conversation or make a request, either stop to engage or ask to meet at another time. Delaying a conversation is better than having a distracted discussion. If you do stop to talk, be sure to ask for a follow-up email as a reminder or set a reminder on your phone to complete an action item.

Multitasking often results in a lack of focus. Schedule time to complete tasks such as responding to emails, and try to complete one task before starting another. Of course, this can be challenging as tasks are added over the course of the day.

To-do lists can help you focus and prioritize tasks. To prioritize people (the *who*) over tasks (the *what*), consider a tiered list. Reserve the top tier or "must do" category for tasks that prioritize the people in your building. Reserve the middle tier or "necessary actions" category for tasks that need to be completed to meet operational or instructional needs. Reserve the bottom tier or "hope to" category for requests or items that aren't time-sensitive. The *what* doesn't matter if the *who* isn't tended to. Take care of your people, and your people will take care of you.

## Conversations as an Investment

Conversations can speak more than just words; they can convey power, control, and emotions as well. Learn to be the second speaker and embrace being the first listener.

Do you initiate conversations in meetings? Do you invite others to launch the conversation? Cuddy (2016) notes, "Talking first says: I know better than you, I am smarter than you, I should speak while you listen" (p. 78). Although waiting to speak may lead the conversation to begin at a different starting point, it does not mean that you've lost control. Allowing the other person to speak first reveals what that person's priority is, which may communicate important information for you to take note of.

Use Covey's (1989) habit "Seek first to understand, then to be understood" (p. 237) to exercise mental presence. Start by trying to understand what is being shared by taking notes, asking clarifying questions, or revoicing key points to clear your mind of your own agenda and focus on the speaker's needs. Additionally, monitor your "airtime." Are you taking up all the available time with your own thoughts, questions, or responses? Do you provide time and space for exchanging thoughts? Remember that interrupting others diminishes the value of their thoughts and inflates the value of your own. Be aware of the urge to interrupt while others are speaking. Consider jotting down important thoughts as they arise to share them once the speaker has concluded.

## The Impact of Emotions

In his book *Social Intelligence*, Daniel Goleman (2006) talks about "the emotional economy" of social interaction, including the points that emotions are contagious and that every interaction has an emotional subtext. Consider how emotions can be shared or spread. When a staff member spends an entire lunch break unloading all of their complaints on others, those on the receiving end may walk out with their own feelings of discontentment, frustration, and negativity. Then the listeners in turn become the negative speakers, further spreading toxic emotions.

As a leader, you influence what emotions are spread with every interaction you have with staff. We've all heard of a contagious laugh, or someone whose smile makes it impossible to not smile too. Emotional currency is conveyed in both words and actions. What you say and do will either come at a cost or pay dividends in the future. Every interaction is a ripple; one can never know how far it will be felt.

Emotional intelligence includes recognizing and managing one's own emotions and recognizing and responding to others' emotions. Awareness is crucial for recognizing emotions. Emotions become thoughts, and thoughts become beliefs and actions, which can positively or negatively affect school culture. Awareness requires effort and intentionality. Emotions fluctuate over the course of the day in response to thoughts, interactions, and events.

Consider how your emotions affect your interactions with staff. As a leader, managing your emotions is critical so that you communicate and interact in meaningful ways. The emotional energy you share with others has the potential to propel positive school culture or crush it. Not only is it important to notice and name your own emotions; it's equally important to be attuned to the emotions of others and how you contribute to those emotions. After you've engaged with a staff member about a concern, does that person walk away wondering if you even care about how the concern makes them feel?

---

**Try This: Develop Your Emotional Awareness and Empathy**

Not everyone has a natural tendency toward emotional awareness and empathy. However, it's possible to consciously develop and improve in this important area of leadership. Here are some ways to do that:

- **Practice nondismissive responses.**
  - Avoid minimizing or dismissing others' emotions.
  - Acknowledge and validate others' feelings to show understanding.
- **Cultivate emotional intelligence.**
  - Read the room attentively, paying attention to nonverbal cues, including eye contact, facial expressions, and body language such as fidgeting or nodding in agreement.
  - Try to understand the unspoken emotions and dynamics in a given situation.

- **Support emotional processing.**
  - Actively engage with others to help them navigate and understand their emotions.
  - Encourage open communication about feelings through leading by example, soliciting feedback, and encouraging reflective practices (e.g., asking, "What emotions is this bringing up for you?").
- **Be an empathetic listener.**
  - Practice active listening to fully comprehend others' perspectives.
  - Reflect on what is being said and show genuine interest in the experiences being shared.
- **Normalize emotions.**
  - Foster an environment in which expressing emotions is considered natural and acceptable.
  - Share your own experiences to create a culture of openness and understanding, focusing on feelings and what you learned from the particular situation. Choose your moments of vulnerability wisely.
- **Encourage self-regulation.**
  - Provide tools and resources for individuals to manage and regulate their own emotions.
  - Promote healthy coping mechanisms and stress-relief strategies. For example, offer to cover teachers' classrooms any time they need a moment to take a break or step away. Sometimes just five minutes is what teachers need when they feel frustrated or are struggling to remain calm and composed.
  - Use walk-and-talks to build connections and release stress. Teachers can change into exercise clothes and walk, talk, and process after school for 30 minutes so they go home with a better mindset.

Approaching emotional awareness and empathy through these actions can contribute to a more supportive and understanding environment. The effort is well worth the time.

# How Feeling Valued Relates to Job Satisfaction

What do you think is the number one reason people change jobs? Why do you think teachers in particular change schools or leave the teaching profession? More money? A promotion? A better position? A school closer to home? Better hours? What stories are we telling ourselves? We have blind spots. It's important to reflect and have honest and hard conversations on this matter.

In reality, the reasons we hear from most teachers for why they're leaving the profession are more psychological than material in nature.

When teachers don't feel connected, don't experience a sense of love and belonging, or don't have their esteem needs met, they're likely to look for employment elsewhere. Unfortunately, those who are most likely to leave are also the most talented. Highly effective teachers can move to another school, or they have transferable skills that make them marketable and appealing to employers outside the field of education.

Once teachers inform a leader that they're leaving, they often give reasons that make it easy to leave on a positive note. In fact, we've never heard of a teacher telling their principal that they're leaving because they just didn't feel connected. But as coaches, here are examples of what we *have* heard from teachers:

- "I feel so defeated and all alone."
- "I just want to be part of a team where _____."
- "I'm going to such-and-such a school where I know so-and-so."
- "It's just not worth it to me anymore. They couldn't pay me enough to stay here and put up with this."
- "I feel like no one cares or appreciates what I do."
- "I need to work for someone who values me."
- "I'm not a rock star."
- "My heart's not in it anymore."
- "I can't work for [the principal]."

Ouch! All of these comments reflect an unmet need for love, belonging, and esteem. Trust and belonging form the core of an emotionally safe environment.

When teachers tell us why they choose to remain at a particular school for a long time or pass up opportunities for promotions, they offer comments such as these:

- "I just couldn't leave my team or teaching partner. We're like a family."
- "My hallway is like a warm hug."
- "I love working here so much that it's worth the drive."
- "I love working for [the principal] so much. I'll be here as long as she is the principal."

- "I am just so grateful to [the principal]. I will never forget what he has done for me."

Unlike the first set of comments, these comments reflect met needs for love, belonging, and esteem. Working in this kind of climate outweighs the inconvenience of a long drive or changing content areas or grade levels. This positive attitude is significant. How can we intentionally cultivate it?

Remember that your teachers are humans with feelings. They give so much of themselves. What can you as a school leader do to create a school culture where your teachers' psychological needs for love, belonging, and esteem are met? You can pay attention to who is isolated and create structures to help them become better connected. You can do the work alongside your teachers. You can position yourself as a learner and join the team. And you can keep your door open, be available, and listen.

## Promoting Love, Belonging, and Esteem Within Your Team

Balancing the acknowledgment of existing staff with the integration of new hires requires thoughtful communication and a commitment to fostering a positive team culture. Actively involving and appreciating your current team can help you create a seamless transition for new staff while reinforcing the value of your existing employees.

Telling current teachers that you just hired a "rock star" candidate makes it likely that the new hire will have to struggle harder for love and belonging and esteem. Why? Because the current teachers may feel devalued and perceive that the leader is giving unwarranted status to the newcomer. Keep in mind that everyone has flaws, and it's always better to undersell and overdeliver. Don't get so enthusiastic about someone who is new that you inadvertently say things that make the teachers who've been doing the work day in and day out feel unappreciated. Current team members, many of whom you may not have hired, may come to believe that you see them as weaker than the new hire. This mistaken conclusion can undermine the collective efficacy of your team and hurt the school climate.

As you introduce new hires to your current staff, be mindful of what you want to convey in regard to your values as a leader. Leverage the hiring of new staff to reflect your vision in action. Following are some suggestions for how to do that.

**Focus on the new hire as a team player and a great fit, and share how the team can provide support.**

Here's how this might sound: "We've hired a 6th grade ELA teacher, and she's eager to meet her new team. I believe that she's going to be a great fit; she seems like a real team player. Because she's coming to us from California, she's going to need your help getting acclimated, and we'll be able to learn from her too. In her interview, she talked about having experience at a school that was focused on schoolwide positive behavior."

**Respect staff as individuals.**

Do not compare teachers. Comparisons can damage relationships between teachers. Remember, we each contribute in unique ways. Guide teachers in reflecting on their practice rather than comparing them. For example, avoid saying something such as this: "Ms. Martin was teaching the same lesson on energy transfer, but she gave students more opportunities to talk, and those checks for understanding allowed her to recognize and respond to student misconceptions sooner." Feedback should not suggest status differences or provoke dissension. Rather, feedback should be specific to the staff member and designed to help move that person forward.

**Always speak about teachers as if they're in the room.**

When a school leader speaks negatively about a teacher or staff member, past or present, or agrees with a negative comment, it erodes trust for everyone in earshot. When Jessica overheard a school leader say, "He drives me crazy" about a staff member, she wondered what was said about her when she wasn't in the room. Her reaction is hardly unique. Any time a school staff member hears a school leader talk about a colleague, they automatically wonder what the school leader thinks and says about them.

### *Give actionable feedback that's specific to a teacher's goals.*

Specificity is key to meaningful feedback. For example, if a teacher's goal is to gather formative data during lessons, focus your feedback on that specific goal. Here's what you might say: "I noticed some students had misconceptions about energy transfer. I wonder where in the lesson we could have asked a question and had students turn and talk with partners so that we could check for understanding earlier in the lesson. Where would you want to do that? What would you ask? Do you think you could work with our instructional coach to plan a lesson with checks for understanding and opportunities for academic discourse within the next week? I'd like to come back and observe again. Let me know which day I should come."

### *Talk with someone, not about someone.*

Talking *with* someone can prevent gossip and hurt feelings. No one likes to be talked *about*, especially if their character is called into question. Hard conversations may be uncomfortable, but that discomfort is shorter-lived than the aftermath created by a resentful staff member who feels mistreated.

### *Vent to the right people.*

When you need to vent, do you talk to those in your small and trusted inner circle or to a broader assortment of other staff members? Make sure your inner circle consists of people who will tell you what you need to hear (like when you have a speck of food between your teeth) and who will guard your secrets. Give them permission to tell you when your ego or unhealed issues are interfering with your ability to see a situation accurately or respond effectively. Remember, feelings are temporary. As the leader, you model for teachers and students how to manage your feelings. You can be both genuine and positive.

### *Consider unintended consequences.*

Although you may not think you talk negatively about teachers, you may be wrong. Here's a cautionary tale. At a school Carrie was involved with, someone wrote an anonymous letter to the principal.

It contained some criticism of the leader and her ideas, and she found it hurtful. Moreover, the principal received it on the final day before winter break—a time when educators are generally exhausted and even the strongest leaders are running on fumes. Over the next few weeks, the principal speculated as to who had written the letter, including naming specific teachers. Talking to teachers and asking about certain colleagues was like spraying oxygen on a fire. The negativity expressed in the letter grew, and some of the accusations in the letter that some teachers initially disagreed with began to seem valid. The principal's reaction reinforced what was becoming an adversarial relationship between administrator and teachers.

## Promoting Belonging and Esteem for Historically Underrepresented Staff

It's not unusual for teachers from underrepresented cultures to feel isolated when none of their colleagues are like them. Such feelings are real. What concrete steps can district and school leaders take to ensure that these teachers have their needs met in the areas of love, belonging, and esteem? What structures and systems need to be put in place to intentionally support teachers? Effective schools foster a web of relationships among staff so that everyone feels connected and supported. What follows are some ways to work toward this important goal.

### *Model embracing diverse experiences, thoughts, and cultures.*

Ask questions. Stay curious. Learn about diverse cultures, experiences, and beliefs. Celebrate diversity with your words and actions. Your teachers will consciously and unconsciously mimic what they see you doing.

### *Keep students at the center, keep your door open, and build strong relationships.*

Stay open and focused on kids to build the kinds of relationships with teachers that foster trust. All teachers, including those who are culturally underrepresented on a staff, benefit from being able to trust that they can approach school leaders and call out needs for change that will benefit students. Respond to teachers with support and encourage them to have open conversations with you, take initiative, and advocate on behalf of student needs. Dixon and colleagues (2019) note, "Administrators build relationships with their staff by being responsive, transparent, and communicating effectively" (p. 22).

### Intentionally leverage protocols, room arrangements, and assigning of groups and tasks to promote inclusivity.

Consider how to proactively be inclusive and include everyone's voice. Discussion protocols can help avoid situations where some people always share and some opt out of sharing. Strategical staff placement during professional development or other group activities can "shake up" friend groups and forestall echo chambers where everyone has the same viewpoint. Consider assigning seats and then having everyone relocate every 20 minutes or so to provide opportunities to connect and engage with diverse viewpoints. Diversifying the participants in conversations can cultivate a more robust exchange of ideas. At the same time, do not assume that everyone will welcome others. Use specific protocols and seating arrangements to promote equity and create a culture where everyone's voice has value.

### Plan monthly team-building activities.

To create a work environment where teachers feel comfortable being their authentic, whole selves, they need opportunities to build relationships. To feel safe and have a sense of belonging, they need strong ties with the people they interact with daily. Building those relationships fosters trust. It's important to make time for team-building activities that go beyond icebreakers.

Participating in team-building activities can help educators better understand one another's strengths, preferences, and working styles. This deeper level of connection and appreciation can lead to improved communication, a stronger sense of community, and more effective collaboration. When educators feel like a cohesive unit, they are more likely to support one another, share resources and ideas, and work together toward common educational goals. This ultimately makes the team more productive, enhances job satisfaction, and enhances student outcomes.

Ask yourself, "How am I taking advantage of collaborative tasks to affirm teachers' identity and authentic self? How am I accepting people and showing love toward them?" As Dixon and colleagues (2019) explain, "Principals realize that relationships are extremely important for underrepresented teachers, and building a family atmosphere among staff is foundational to retaining underrepresented teachers" (p. 21).

### Acknowledge that everyone needs a mentor.

No one thrives on an island. Don't expect people to experience connection, love, and belonging and to have their esteem needs met while residing on a metaphorical island. Pair culturally underrepresented teachers with mentors with whom they have something in common. People seek connection. If they can't find it at your school, they will look for it at another place of work.

### Administer an inclusion index survey.

Consider turning the following statements, taken from the Gartner Inclusion Index, as cited in Romansky and colleagues (2021), into a survey to check the inclusivity of your school culture:

1. Fair treatment: Employees at my organization who help the organization achieve its strategic objectives are rewarded and recognized fairly.
2. Integrating differences: Employees at my organization respect and value each other's opinions.
3. Decision making: Members of my team fairly consider ideas and suggestions offered by other team members.
4. Psychological safety: I feel welcome to express my true feelings at work.
5. Trust: Communication we receive from the organization is honest and open.
6. Belonging: People in my organization care about me.

7. Diversity: Managers at my organization are as diverse as the broader workforce. (paras. 9–15)

Have staff respond to each statement using a Likert scale with a range from "strongly agree" to "strongly disagree." Use the results to address blind spots and respond accordingly.

See Figure 4.3 for a sample worksheet describing three scenarios, with space to enter ideas for a plan for how to deal with each. Use it as a starting point for considering how you might address similar situations in your school.

FIGURE 4.3

**Planning for Diversity**

| Scenario | Plan |
|---|---|
| You hire a male teacher to join an all-female elementary school faculty. What steps do you take to ensure his needs for belonging and esteem are met? | |
| You hire a Black teacher to join an all-white faculty. What steps do you take to ensure the newcomer's needs for belonging and esteem are met? How might you increase cultural diversity in your staff? | |
| You hire a staff member with hearing impairment. What steps do you take to ensure the person's needs for belonging and esteem are met? | |

# Appreciation as an Investment

Being appreciated makes us feel valued for our thoughts, efforts, and actions. A school leader who prioritizes people not only values staff but also explicitly expresses appreciation for them. In *The 5 Languages of Appreciation in the Workplace,* Gary Chapman and Paul White (2019) share findings from research about job satisfaction. They report that more than 80 percent of employees say they're motivated to work harder when their boss shows appreciation for their work.

It's important to recognize that rewards are not the same as appreciation. Allowing teachers to wear jeans and scheduling "dress down days" do not communicate the value of staff members' work. In fact, some teachers find it offensive to dress unprofessionally for their job. Moreover, it can feel condescending to teachers to reward them in the same way you might reward students.

To express genuine appreciation, be sure that your effort is not a one-size-fits-all approach that conveys minimal effort and ignores people's individuality. For example, an appreciation event that features food and beverages with no regard to food allergies, dietary restrictions, or health preferences won't necessarily be well received. Remember that adults need choice.

One way to honor the need for choice is to become familiar with staff members' "languages of appreciation"—the topic of Chapman and White's book. The languages that they identify are (1) words of affirmation, (2) quality time, (3) acts of service, (4) tangible gifts, and (5) physical touch. Most people *show* appreciation in the language in which they like to *receive* appreciation. As a result, many school leaders make great efforts to show appreciation but don't get the desired results because they don't trouble themselves to identify their teachers' languages of appreciation. One way to address the disconnect is by asking staff members to take an online assessment tool that Chapman and White have developed, called the Motivation by Appreciation Inventory (an MBA Inventory specifically targeted at schools can be found at https://shop.appreciationatwork.com/collections/mba-inventory/products/expanded-mba-inventory-school). You can use the results and suggestions to personalize your efforts to show appreciation.

Let's take a closer look at the five languages of appreciation.

### Words of Affirmation

In a school setting, words of affirmation may include praise for accomplishments, affirmation of character, and acknowledgment of positive personality traits. When using words of affirmation with staff, consider what will be the most effective approach. Should the delivery be one-on-one, in front of others, in written form (e.g., a note left after a classroom visit), or in a public setting? Beware of hollow or insincere praise, which may have a negative effect on someone who values sincere words of affirmation.

## Quality Time

To acknowledge team members who feel appreciated when you spend time with them, adjust your schedule to make time for quality conversations, shared experiences, small-group dialogue, or working in close physical proximity with coworkers. During this shared time, listen for feelings expressed as well as thoughts, and affirm people's feelings even if you don't agree with their conclusions. Observe body language, and resist the impulse to interrupt. Be aware of making eye contact and being present physically, unencumbered by your cell phone or other distractions.

Other ways to spend quality time with staff members during school hours include having lunch together in the school cafeteria, taking a walk around the school grounds, or observing a class together and discussing it afterward. These interactions provide valuable opportunities to build relationships, offer mentorship, and discuss school-related goals in an informal setting. However, it's important to be mindful of how these interactions might be perceived by others. To avoid any perceptions of favoritism, ensure that you make such opportunities available to all staff members and that you spend your time equitably with team members. Transparency and inclusivity in these interactions help to maintain trust and respect within your school community.

## Acts of Service

Acts of service can take the form of helping with tasks, such as tidying up classrooms or work areas, cleaning up after a dance, or taking over coverage for lunch, bus, or parking lot duty. Beware of conveying a negative attitude by offering an act of service begrudgingly. Show up with a smile and do the work alongside the employee or, in the case of duty coverage, by yourself. If you aren't sure how to do a job, ask. Your question will show that you're a learner.

## Tangible Gifts

For those whose language of appreciation is tangible gifts, be sure to solicit input about what type of gift they would appreciate. Not bothering to personalize gift giving is a missed opportunity. Consider having teachers and staff complete a list of suggestions so you have ideas for gifts. Beware of ignoring cultural differences by, for example, giving everyone a Christmas gift and assuming the gesture will be universally appreciated. Think about what kind of gifts will connect with your staff's sense of school spirit.

## Physical Touch

You may be wondering about physical touch, which is not included in the Motivating by Appreciation Inventory mentioned earlier. Physical touch is not an appropriate primary language of appreciation at a workplace. However, handshakes, fist bumps, and high fives are acceptable ways to greet colleagues or celebrate a job well done.

---

### Try This: Check In to Deter Turnover

Staff turnover is inevitable. Some circumstances are simply outside our control. However, school leaders can take actionable steps to invest in teachers and encourage teammates to invest in one another. Here are some suggestions:

- **Solicit feedback**. The next time you have the unpleasant surprise of a highly effective teacher transferring to another school or leaving the field of education altogether, try asking them, "Is there anything I could do that would make you stay?" If the teacher hesitates, is reluctant to answer, or says, "No, it's not you," try following up with something such as this: "I believe that feedback is a gift. I really value you, and your insights could help me grow. I want to keep top talent like you so our students benefit from the quality instructional experiences you provide. If you don't feel comfortable answering right now, I can give you some time to think about it. Would it be OK if I ask you again before you leave, or would you share responses in an exit interview?"
- **Administer a survey.** Have employees take the school version of the MBA Inventory mentioned earlier. Although this assessment tool is not free, it's an investment that provides you with detailed and useful information. As a school leader, you can use the results to communicate appreciation using the preferred language of each individual staff member and avoid wasting time and energy on misaligned efforts. After the initial expense and the time spent getting responses from the entire faculty, the effort will involve only the maintenance cost of onboarding new hires.

- **Take a pulse.** Send out a survey that asks just one question—"Do you feel valued?"—and allows respondents to remain anonymous.

## Empathy Episode

Read the following Empathy Episode and imagine what it would feel like to be in the teacher's position. Then use the reflection questions to consider leadership blind spots and how to remedy them.

> You have worked up the courage to invite your principal to visit your 7th grade science class. You know how busy your principal has been. She always seems stressed, so you've debated whether to add one more thing to the list of things you'd like her to observe. However, over the past two weeks, your more than 130 students have been working on a problem-based unit that involves designing solutions for a local company. Representatives from the company are coming to the school to listen to student presentations of their solutions. Student engagement is at an all-time high, and they're demonstrating mastery on several standards and using essential skills in communication to share their ideas. You spent summer professional development time developing this unit and continued to refine it on your own time because you were so excited about it.
>
> You emailed your principal an invitation a week in advance but received no response. You decide it's worth mentioning in person the morning of the event because you know the principal will be in the building. Your principal says, "I'll try" as she walks down the hall to handle the next thing on her endless to-do list. You watch your classroom door all day, hoping your principal will walk through. It never happens. Although it's been a great day observing your students present to professionals, you can't seem to shake the undercurrent of disappointment.

### Reflection Questions

- How could the school leader in the scenario have capitalized on the opportunity to make meaningful connections with students and the science teacher?
- What can school leaders in general do to make people their top priority?

When staff invite school leaders into their classroom, they're seeking a response such as feedback, affirmation, appreciation, or validation. School leaders who don't accept these invitations are missing opportunities to value staff and show appreciation. They're also communicating that something else is more important than the learning that's happening in the classroom. The lack of clarity in the answer "I'll try" instead of "yes" or "no" left the teacher in the scenario anxiously watching the door. This emotional distraction could negatively affect the experience for students or the teacher's ability to engage with the community partners. Another missed opportunity was that the principal could have spent time networking with community partners and showing appreciation for their presence and their contribution to the school.

Using a different approach, the principal could have declined the invitation with an explanation of a previous commitment or scheduling conflict and expressed gratitude for the teacher's efforts. The principal could have invited the teacher to debrief and reflect on the experience afterward, and she could have sent a thank-you communication to the community partners.

The scenario illustrates the importance of addressing Maslow's hierarchy of needs in providing a safe environment, creating a sense of love and belonging, and conveying esteem by showing appreciation. One of the best ways to prioritize people is to create a psychologically safe environment where staff feel safe, soothed, secure, and seen. Consistently showing up and being reliable in times of both success and struggle builds trust. Trust is a foundational element of any healthy relationship, and it contributes to a sense of security. Being present and showing up for staff fosters love and belonging. Showing up involves active listening, where individuals fully engage with each other's thoughts, feelings, and experiences. This attentive presence communicates that others matter and are valued, contributing to a sense of care and understanding. Showing appreciation fulfills a staff member's desire for recognition, respect, and a sense of accomplishment. It signifies that their work and presence are recognized and have a positive impact on the team or organization.

## How Will You Commit?

- What strategies from this chapter are you committed to implementing?

- Who can help you implement these strategies?
- What outcome do you want to see as a result of implementing these strategies?

## Summary

In this chapter, we discussed how to prioritize people over tasks. A people-centric focus contributes to the development of a positive workplace culture. Being present both physically and mentally communicates to staff that they are valued. Employees who feel prioritized and appreciated will likely be more motivated and productive. Intentional and personalized demonstrations of appreciation are more likely to positively affect staff than generic acts. Prioritizing the people in your building creates the foundation for investing in people, the topic we will discuss in Chapter 5.

# 5

# Believing in Your Team

*About five years ago, my current principal encouraged me to apply for a district leadership development cohort to get on a path to leadership or administration in our district. I was, and still am, very resistant to this idea, as this is not my ambition professionally; however, it was a confidence booster that she believed I was capable of leading others to do great things.*

—Jennifer Clark, teacher

Do we genuinely believe that all teachers in our schools can be successful? Sure! That's why we hired them. But do our actions and words reflect our faith in them and the value we see in them, the way Jennifer's principal's do? The second question might be harder to answer. This vital part of our work might get away from us as we go through our intensely busy days. In a 2013 TED Talk, longtime educator Rita Pierson famously declared, "Every child needs a champion." We believe every *educator* deserves a champion too.

As educators, we know our collective efficacy is far greater than our individual impact. If we can get everyone rowing in the same direction toward the same goal, we can overcome challenges and do far more good for students than one person could ever do alone. Developing a team that values collaboration over competition and that honors and employs individuals' strengths and input is difficult but worth the effort.

Team members who know they are valued and belong are more likely to invest in the organization. Trust is fundamental for fostering love and a sense of belonging in interpersonal relationships. When trust is present, it creates a foundation of safety, reliability, and emotional connection that encourages individuals to be vulnerable and authentic with each other. This openness fosters a deeper understanding of the problems and needs of students, families, and teachers and allows the real obstacles to be addressed and removed.

When we acknowledge and value the abilities of our colleagues, we hold them in high esteem. In the process, we're also developing our own self-esteem, competence, and confidence. When people feel that others have confidence in their abilities, value their contributions, and believe in their potential, their self-esteem and self-confidence can be significantly enhanced, enabling them to bring the best version of themselves to work. When educators experience belief from leaders and each other, they're more likely to reciprocate that belief. This dynamic contributes to a positive and reinforcing cycle of mutual support and encouragement that positively affects students, families, preservice teachers, and current educators.

So how do we ensure that the talented educators we're honored to serve know that we recognize them as unique team members whose growth we want to support? We demonstrate that we believe in them and build their competence and confidence. Take a moment to complete the self-assessment in Figure 5.1 to get a sense of where your school stands in this regard.

## The Pygmalion Effect

The *Pygmalion effect* is shorthand for living up to high expectations, just because those expectations exist. According to Dan Pilat and Sekoul Krastev, co-founders of The Decision Lab, a behavioral science and design consulting firm,

> The Pygmalion effect happens because as social creatures, we are influenced by others' expectations. If we expect success from someone else, we are likely to give them greater support in order to help them achieve that success. Similarly, if we

believe someone has high expectations of us, we will work harder to meet those expectations. Expectations act as a prophecy because they become motivators for hard work. (n.d., para. 46)

FIGURE 5.1

**Belief in Staff Self-Assessment**

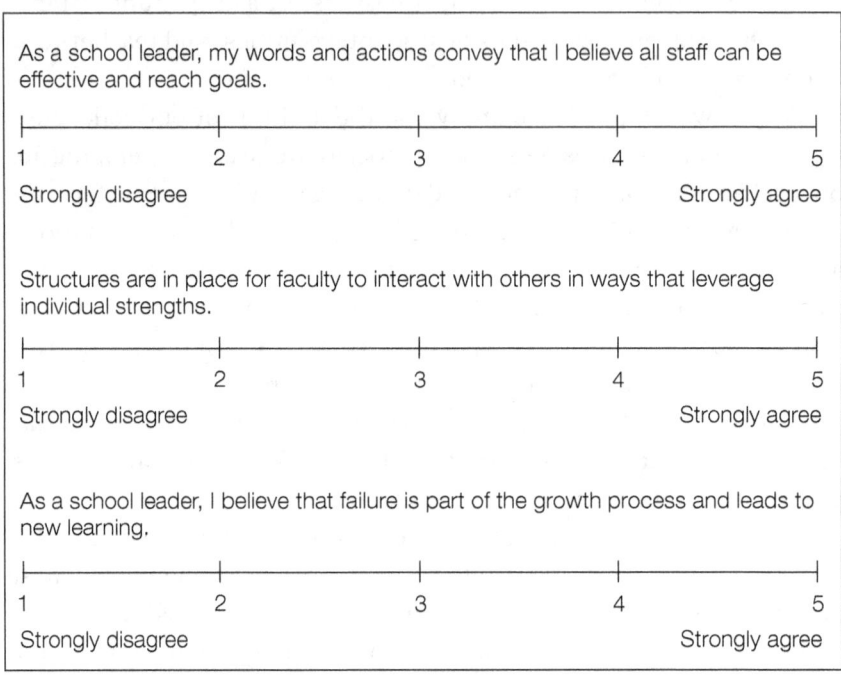

We would further add that negative expectations produce negative results. If we're not expected to perform, it's unlikely that we will. School leaders can harness the Pygmalion effect to support their staff to be their best selves. Believing others can achieve is rooted in the subconscious and manifested in what we say and do.

It's not uncommon for school leaders to emphasize to their faculty the importance of believing in their students. However, these leaders sometimes fail to align their actions with their words by modeling their expectations with regard to teachers.

A school principal's belief in a teacher as a valuable team member fulfills the teacher's need for belongingness and esteem, two components of Maslow's hierarchy. At the highest level of Maslow's hierarchy is self-actualization, which involves reaching one's full potential and personal growth. When a school principal believes in a teacher, their support provides a foundation for self-actualization. Belief from the principal encourages teachers to strive for continuous improvement, take risks, and explore innovative ideas. It creates an environment where teachers feel empowered to develop their skills, embrace new challenges, and pursue their professional goals.

The Conscious Competence Learning Model, or Four Stages of Competence, was first introduced by management trainer Martin M. Broadwell in the 1960s. The model outlines four stages of learning:

1. *Unconscious incompetence.* The learner does not yet know what they don't know.
2. *Conscious incompetence.* The learner becomes aware of what they don't know.
3. *Conscious competence.* The learner knows how to do something but must focus consciously on their actions.
4. *Unconscious competence.* The learner has practiced enough that the skill becomes second nature and can be performed effortlessly. (Adams & Riding, 2006)

The conscious competence stage is crucial for teachers because it represents a phase where they are aware of their knowledge and skills and are actively and intentionally applying them in their practice. This stage allows teachers to be reflective and deliberate in their teaching methods, which is essential for their growth and development as educators (Broadwell, 1969). Teachers with conscious competence are equipped with the knowledge and skills to make informed instructional choices and possess the ability to articulate the rationale behind their decisions. This stage allows teachers to confidently navigate the complex and ever-evolving landscape of education, ensuring that their teaching practices align with the best interests of their students.

School leaders play a crucial role in fostering conscious competence among their teachers. Providing opportunities for professional development, encouraging reflective practices, and promoting a culture of ongoing learning can support teachers in their journey toward conscious competence. This stage benefits individual teachers and enhances the overall quality of education as teachers become more effective in facilitating student growth and achievement. And remember, the people you lead are watching not only how you respond to them but also how you respond to others.

When Jessica was in her fourth year of teaching and her first year at a new school, she had moments of self-doubt about her abilities to be an effective educator. She juggled the challenges of moving to a new city, learning district and school expectations, and working in an unfamiliar school community. During this time, she received support from both the school-based and district-level coaches. They worked to integrate Jessica's prior experience with a writing strategy used in her previous school with the new district's curriculum. Toward the end of the school year, the district-level coach encouraged Jessica to submit a proposal to share the writing strategy at a local literacy conference. She remembers feeling she was not qualified to speak at a conference, but after some nudging and encouragement, she applied and was selected to present. Because one person believed in her, Jessica started to believe more in herself.

One way school leaders can show they believe in a teacher is to elevate promising or best practices observed in the teacher's classroom. Teaching can be isolating, and teachers often don't see how other teachers do things. By inviting teachers to share their practices, school leaders convey a deep belief in those practices, and other teachers can expand their repertoire of best practices, develop, and grow, increasing student learning.

> **Try This: Promote Peer Observations**
>
> When observing in classrooms, identify the best or most promising practices you would like to see more frequently. Name these practices and clearly explain what makes them effective. Offer monthly 15-minute sessions for teachers to share these practices with one another (consider multiple sessions each month so teachers can fit attendance into their schedules). Arrange dates and times for teachers to observe the practice enacted in the

classroom. Provide coverage so colleagues can observe each other, or have teachers go during their planning time. In future classroom observations, note whether more teachers are employing the promising or best practices.

Inviting staff to learn from each other promotes collaboration over competition. When individuals collaborate and contribute to a team or group effort, they are rewarded by others acknowledging and validating their contributions. Recognition for one's skills, ideas, and efforts can positively affect self-esteem.

## Uncovering Strengths and Potential

Every staff member is unique in terms of strengths, experiences, and potential. Often individuals put themselves in a metaphorical box, limiting themselves. Moreover, they sometimes overlook their own strengths in favor of dwelling on weaker areas. When people understand who they are, what their strengths are, and the value they can add to the team, they're more likely to engage and contribute.

Numerous tests, some free of charge and others requiring a fee, are available to help individuals identify their strengths. Most are available online. Consider making such tests available to your staff to help them gain self-knowledge and bring their best selves to the team.

### Try This: Strengths Assessment

Adobe is a company that has been known for creativity and inspiring content creators for years. The Adobe Creative Types test (https://mycreativetype.com/; free) is grounded in the belief that we're all creative and have differing strengths as creative types. Taking the test reveals which creative type you are (out of eight possibilities), describes traits of that type, and identifies an ideal collaborator type. There are nuances, though: A person can have traits that fit more than one type, and what type of collaborator is ideal is not necessarily reciprocal. The test is a great way to unify a team by tapping into everyone's creative strength.

The Enneagram test focuses on discovering personality type (www.enneagraminstitute.com/; $20). It helps people understand their natural tendencies, including what they need most to be productive and what might cause them to disconnect from others. It helps individuals think about how they most often contribute to a team. The test's identifies strengths and potentially unproductive traits for nine personality types. Results include identifying the personality type someone works best with and which type might be challenging to work with. The Enneagram is useful for improving self-awareness and understanding team dynamics.

> The Myers-Briggs Type Indicator, commonly known as the Myers-Briggs test, builds off the work of Carl Jung's theory of psychological types (www.mbtionline.com; $59.95). Its creators, Isabel Briggs Myers and her mother, Katharine Cook Briggs, made the notion of psychological types accessible and applicable to the general public, who were unlikely to understand the academic theory behind them. Initially, the test was used for self-knowledge, but it has expanded to businesses and organizations as a way for individuals to identify their preferences and learn how to work in teams. The 16 personalities are indicated with various combinations of four letters representing components of the type (extraversion/introversion, sensing/intuition, thinking/feeling, judging/perceiving). All types are equal and have their own strengths and weaknesses. This test is excellent for providing insight into your own personality and personal and professional relationships.
>
> Numerous other tests are available and may provide different lenses for uncovering individual strengths. Taking a strengths/personality assessment in a group setting promotes connecting around commonalities and appreciating differences, and may lead to developing a better understanding of how to perform as a team.

## Strategies to Capitalize on Strengths

Once your staff members have identified their individual strengths, it's time for you to put the information to good use. Here are some ideas.

### Designed Groups

At a team-building staff meeting, assign seats and compose teams strategically instead of relying on a random or self-selected approach. You may encounter eye rolls and deep sighs as people realize they've been assigned seats or groups. However, some staff will probably secretly appreciate the change. Design teams in various ways depending on the desired outcome of the activity. For example, include a person from each grade level to include voices that span the entire student learning trajectory. Pair ideal collaborators based on individual creative strengths. Populate teams with a balanced representation of experience.

### Intergenerational Interaction

Create multigenerational groups to address a student-centered problem. As discussed in Chapter 3, generations have their own unique strengths, weaknesses, and perspectives—although, of course, individuals within each generation vary considerably. Think about the diverse contributions that might emerge from having members of more than one generation share ideas for solutions to a problem. We often have tunnel vision based on our experience and generational mindsets. Expanding that narrow view by collaboratively solving problems with others can yield positive results for students and staff.

### Collaborative Contrasts

Plan an activity that pairs staff members who display opposite (complementary) attributes based on one of the inventories. Conversations and idea generation are more robust when diverse thinkers work together. Like-minded or homogeneous groups can create an echo chamber with a narrow lens and lots of blind spots.

## From Unconscious to Conscious Competence

Earlier we described the concept of conscious competence. Unconscious competence refers to teachers who are good at what they do but may not fully understand why. As coaches, Carrie and Jessica have had debriefings with teachers who have no idea why a lesson they presented went well. They acknowledge their success, but when pressed to name a particular move or instructional strategy to explain the catalyst, they often shrug or struggle to find an answer. Many teachers make skilled moves and strategic choices without even realizing it. Mentoring and coaching can support these staff in moving from unconscious to conscious competence, which fosters intentional practice and refinement of educational approaches.

Leaders can also provide specific feedback to promote consciousness. Teachers must be made aware of what they're doing right so they can replicate it. Positive reinforcement contributes to a strong sense of competence. As a school leader, leverage other leaders and peers in the building to increase awareness and recognize competency in practice. Mentors and coaches can frame feedback by saying, "That *[move or strategy]* is resulting in *[effect]*. This is important because...." Teachers want to be competent, and being acknowledged for doing something well builds confidence.

> **Try This: Use POP Postcards for Feedback**
>
> The Point Out Practice (POP) Postcard strategy is a quick way to name a move or strategy that yields positive results without disrupting class or requiring a follow-up conversation. It's a form of feedback that's accessible to everyone. However, to make sense, it needs a common language for teaching moves and strategies. The moves and strategies can be printed on the postcard for efficiency, but don't overlook the importance of personalizing the feedback.
>
> Too often, we're so focused on fixing weaknesses that we overlook staff members' strengths. Ironically, staff are likely able to name numerous areas in which they could improve. They don't usually need us to tell them what could be better; they already know. What they need is to be told what went well. It's OK to name the same teacher move or strategy more than once. Doing so shows consistency in application. However, it's also OK to encourage teachers to expand their repertoire of moves and strategies.

## At Every Age and Stage

Creating connections among staff members can yield immense value. When veteran and new teachers connect, they exchange energy as well as knowledge—and the flow goes both ways. New teachers bring excitement and fresh ideas to the relationship. Veteran teachers bring ideas based on experiences and a sense of calm in a stressful job. Connecting should not be limited to the bookends of teachers' careers, however. Mid-career educators can connect with new and veteran teachers to avoid complacency and stagnation.

The professional lifespan of most teachers follows an unspoken bell curve. Some leaders might perceive the beginning and end of a teacher's career to be times an educator has the least to offer. This attitude creates a doubly negative perspective for second-career teachers, who are both new to the career and not 20-something. A balanced staff benefits all educators. When staff composition tips toward the majority being veteran teachers, the imbalance brings a risk of complacency, disengagement, or singularity of thought. When it tips toward the majority being new teachers, the risk is high enthusiasm but a lack of practicality. When a majority of teachers have 5 to 15 years of experience, the risk is competitiveness over collaboration.

Reviewing the years of experience across your staff members is worth a closer look. Here are some reflection questions to help you analyze the situation:

- What's the average number of years of experience for your current staff?
- What's the distribution of years of experience among your current staff?
- How are the teachers in their 20s treated? How are teachers in their 60s treated?
- What percentage of staff are newly graduated from college or beginning their second career?

Remember that being older, younger, more experienced, less experienced, or a second-career teacher does not automatically correlate with irrelevance or having less to share.

When Carrie served as an area learning coach supporting 19 schools, she worked with instructional coaches at each. Within the cohort were veterans with many more years of experience than Carrie herself, as well as first-year instructional coaches. The time period was also noteworthy, as it covered the time when COVID-related school closures were a challenge. Carrie found that by intentionally partnering novice and veteran coaches, both groups benefited and expressed an increased sense of belonging and community. She called each coach individually and explained how she envisioned their mentor–mentee relationship would work. In some cases, the coach-to-coach connections also led to increased collaboration between the principals of the schools.

The value of educator-to-educator connections cannot be underestimated. Leaders have the unique opportunity to develop systems and structures that help educators of all ages and stages build trusting relationships with each other.

## Believing in Those Not Like You

Believing in employees who aren't like you is fundamental to fostering diversity, equity, and inclusion in the workplace. Embracing differences and recognizing each individual's value to the team can lead to a more innovative, collaborative, and supportive work environment. Colleagues with different backgrounds, experiences, and perspectives bring diverse viewpoints to the table. Believing in each of them means recognizing the richness that diversity adds to problem solving, decision making, and creativity.

Ultimately, we can all have a positive effect on students' lives. Believing in the capabilities of all staff allows you to tap into a wealth of knowledge and skills that can broaden your own understanding and skill set. Embracing staff who aren't like you fosters cultural competence by enabling the understanding and appreciation of different perspectives. In turn, this can lead to more effective communication, collaboration, and relationship building within the team and with external stakeholders. A team that believes in the strengths of each member, regardless of differences, is likely to have healthier and more effective dynamics. This supportive environment encourages open communication, trust, and collaboration.

Believing in staff who aren't like you is a cornerstone of diversity and inclusion and a strategic approach to building high-performing and resilient teams. It recognizes each team member's unique strengths and contributions and fosters an environment where everyone can thrive and succeed.

## When Doubt Is Present

What do leaders do when they doubt a staff member's ability? As a school leader, you may sometimes worry that a teacher hasn't yet built the capacity to be effective in the classroom, and with valid reasons. What makes it difficult for you to believe in this teacher? Reflect on the reasons behind the doubt. Are there any biases, personal conflicts, or miscommunications that might be influencing your perception? Be honest with yourself. Once you've identified specific reasons, develop a way forward. If one of the reasons is that the teacher has not been responsive to actionable feedback given on other occasions, then communicate that point to the teacher. If the teacher struggles in the area of educator-to-student connections, drill down and identify the specific behaviors contributing to how the teacher is perceived by students. Identifying the root cause of doubt allows you to move to corrective action instead of indulging a negative mindset.

Unconscious incompetence contributes to doubt. Staff who are unconsciously incompetent in certain areas may struggle with performance, leading to doubts about their overall effectiveness. Leaders may question their ability to handle responsibilities and contribute to the school. They may doubt the person's suitability for a role if there is a significant misalignment between the current skill level and the expectations for the position. Furthermore, unconscious incompetence can affect team dynamics if the individual's lack of awareness or skills hinders collaborative efforts. This situation may raise a leader's concerns about the person's ability to work effectively within a team.

Don't allow doubt to linger. Following are some specific ways to address such a situation.

## Collect Data and Communicate

When you have doubts about a specific practice, take time to observe the teacher. Document the practice and any reactions to clarify the root cause of your concern and its implications. Expressing your preferences and displaying emotions are not likely to be well received by the teacher; you cannot simply say, "I don't like this" because you would not have done it that way. Nevertheless, be sure to communicate your concerns to the teacher. It's unfair to expect staff to change behavior or improve practices if they're unaware of the need for change.

Here's a sentence frame to help communicate about an area for growth: "When you *[name behavior]*, it results in *[state implications]* and affects *[identify who is affected]*." Give the teacher actionable feedback. Be as clear and specific as possible with examples, but focus on future improvement rather than past mistakes. When possible, frame the feedback to acknowledge strengths as well as areas for growth. Is there a way to leverage an existing strength to address a deficit? Position yourself as a researcher and ask genuine questions to understand the intentions behind the teacher's actions. Asking questions helps test your own assumptions and reduce bias.

## Offer Support and Resources

Provide mentoring, professional development, training, and coaching to teachers who need assistance. If your building is fortunate enough to have an instructional coach who can partner with this teacher, be sure to offer the coach's support. Depending on the need and the supports available, select the best option for growing and developing this teacher. In addition, commit to the suggested support and make a plan to provide it. Set goals, action steps, and a timeline for improvement. Be clear about success criteria, how often you will observe in the classroom, and the cadence of feedback the teacher can expect. Conduct regular check-ins. These should be one-on-one conversations with the teacher, and they should allow for revisions to the schedule of support. Your goal should be for the teacher to leave the check-in meeting feeling inspired and eager to get to work, not negative, defeated, hopeless, and unproductive.

## Foster Collaboration

Partner the teacher with a colleague in situations where teamwork and mutual respect can help contribute to the teacher's growth. Many teachers benefit from collaborative partnerships. The collaboration may need to extend beyond your school to other schools in the district or area. Connecting the teacher and colleague with a specific goal will make the collaboration purposeful and likely to yield results. Collaborate with district-level support, if available, to help with individual teacher development. Sometimes an expert outside the building can provide just the right support at the right moment. If your district has content-specific leads or people in positions that can assist this teacher, ask for help.

## Maintain Professionalism and Fairness

Professionalism, fairness, and a supportive attitude toward the teacher are crucial. Creating a growth-oriented environment is essential, even when you may not initially believe in a teacher. Carrie's experience as an instructional coach provides an example. A teacher who had previously taught at a local private high school was struggling in his 6th grade classroom. His teaching style seemed more appropriate for a high school setting, and he found it difficult to organize instruction effectively for the younger students he was now teaching. Frustration and some misunderstandings occurred between the teacher and the students, and Carrie was concerned about whether the teacher was willing and ready to make the necessary changes to improve outcomes for all. She engaged in a coaching cycle with the teacher, working closely with him for the remainder of the school year. As a result, he showed tremendous growth in his planning and delivery of instruction, including incorporating stopping points to check for understanding, using strategic questioning, and increasing structured student discourse. He was one of Carrie's most enjoyable teachers to coach because of his sense of humor and receptivity.

Ultimately the teacher moved on to a high school teaching position, and his and Carrie's professional paths have crossed numerous times. Although Carrie knew the struggling teacher was not completely suited for teaching 6th graders—and the teacher himself was also frustrated—by being fair and professional, she was able to support him in a way that honored his strengths and helped students. The simple reality was that the teacher was going to be in that classroom with students for at least the remainder of the year, so it was imperative to provide support and believe in his ability to grow.

Remember, as the school leader, your ultimate goal is to help teachers develop their skills, regain confidence, and improve their instructional practices to benefit themselves and their students. Just as students in the classroom are watching how the teacher deals with challenging students or students who struggle to grasp new learning, teachers are watching you as the school leader to see how you respond when teachers underperform.

## Checking Your Ego: It's Not About You

Ego can significantly impede effective leadership by influencing behavior, decision making, and interpersonal relationships. Leaders who are overly focused on their own ideas may be less likely to consider alternative perspectives, hindering innovation and growth. Ego-driven leaders may find it challenging to admit when they're wrong or have made a mistake. This reluctance to acknowledge errors can erode trust and make it difficult for the team to learn from setbacks. Moreover, ego-driven leaders may be prone to taking credit for successes while deflecting blame onto others for failures.

Effective leadership requires self-awareness, humility, and the ability to prioritize the collective goals of the team or organization over personal ego. Leaders who can manage their egos and foster a collaborative and inclusive environment are more likely to inspire trust and success within their teams.

As a leader, letting go of control can feel counterintuitive. However, in Ken Blanchard and Randy Conley's 2022 book *Simple Truths of Leadership: 52 Ways to Be a Servant Leader and Build Trust*, the 45th truth is "The opposite of trust is not distrust—it's control" (p. 107). Control undermines trust because it communicates a lack of faith in the capabilities and judgment of others. It implies that you do not believe your team members can make decisions, take ownership, or contribute meaningfully to the organization's goals. Micromanagement leads to disengagement, decreased motivation, and a sense of disempowerment among team members. Servant leaders prioritize the growth and success of their team, empowering them to make decisions, take risks, and learn from their experiences. This approach fosters a sense of trust because individuals feel valued, respected, and empowered to contribute their unique perspectives and skills.

---

**Try This: Design Professional Learning with—Not for—Others**

Show trust in your team by sharing the responsibility of designing professional learning. Who better to co-create the experience than those who will be participating? Collaboratively planning professional learning involves engaging a team of educators to collectively design, implement, and evaluate professional development activities.

What follows is a step-by-step guide for designing professional development with, not for, the staff. By following these steps, you can create a learning experience that addresses the unique needs of educators on your team and contributes to continuous improvement in teaching and learning.

***1. Form a diverse planning team that includes teachers, administrators, instructional coaches, and other relevant stakeholders.***

Ensure representation from different grade levels and subject areas. Establish norms and agreements that guide the collaborative planning process, including expectations for participation, communication, and decision making within the team. Create an environment that values and encourages different perspectives. Ensure that all team members feel comfortable sharing their ideas and experiences. This diversity can enrich the professional learning experience.

**2. Determine needs and goals.**

Gather input from teachers through surveys, focus groups, or interviews to understand their professional development needs. Use this information to inform the design of the learning experience. Clearly articulate the goals and objectives for the professional learning. Identify the intended outcomes and how they align with broader educational objectives and the needs of the participants. Build in time for reflection throughout the planning process. Encourage team members to reflect on their own teaching practices and consider how professional learning can be adapted to various contexts.

**3. Select facilitators and resources.**

Identify facilitators who have expertise in the chosen topic or instructional strategy. Select resources such as readings, videos, and case studies to support the learning objectives. Ensure that facilitators are well prepared to lead sessions effectively. Offer professional development opportunities for facilitators to enhance their skills and align their approaches with professional learning goals.

**4. Co-create professional learning sessions.**

Collaboratively design interactive, engaging, and relevant sessions for the participants. Consider incorporating hands-on activities, discussions, and opportunities for reflection. Develop a flexible schedule that accommodates different learning preferences and constraints. Consider offering a mix of in-person and virtual sessions to cater to diverse needs. Before the official launch, pilot a session or two to gather participant feedback and make necessary adjustments. This iterative process ensures that professional learning is responsive to the needs of educators.

**5. Gather feedback and adjust.**

Plan to implement ongoing support structures such as follow-up sessions, mentoring, or communities of practice to sustain the impact of the professional learning beyond the initial sessions. Establish an evaluation process to assess the effectiveness of the professional learning. Collect feedback from participants and the planning team, and use this information to adjust for future iterations.

# The Freedom to Fail

A psychologically safe environment is one where individuals feel comfortable taking risks, expressing their ideas, and making mistakes without fear of negative consequences. Failure is part of learning and growth, and it's essential to creating a culture where the staff knows you believe in them even when things go wrong. Innovation happens in environments where educators feel safe to try methods that may not succeed. If they fear that a failed attempt will permanently ruin their reputation, they're unlikely to innovate.

Never underestimate the magnitude of what happens after teachers take a risk and learn that their ideas do not work. How you respond when plans go awry or the desired outcome is not achieved reveals whether or not the school is a safe place to learn and grow. People will remember how you treated them at their worst. They also watch how you treat others who mess up or underperform. They're looking for indications of safety and trust. In an environment where failure is accepted, individuals are less afraid of punishment or negative consequences for their mistakes. This reduction in fear allows team members to be more authentic, express themselves openly, and contribute without feeling anxiety related to the possibility of retribution. As a leader, you will reap the reward of innovative ideas that can help to achieve your school's mission and vision.

Paradoxically, failure can play a crucial role in building confidence and competence. Although it may initially shake one's self-assurance, most people will agree that they gleaned their most valuable learning experiences and growth from failure. Here's how failure can contribute to building confidence and competence.

- **Failure helps you learn from mistakes.** Failure offers a chance to analyze mistakes, understand their underlying causes, and learn from them. It provides an opportunity to test different strategies, methodologies, or approaches. You can refine your methods by experimenting and adapting in the face of failure and identifying what works best. This iterative process of trial and error helps build competence by gradually honing skills and approaches.
- **Failure helps you develop resilience and perseverance.** Failure often requires you to face disappointment and adversity. As you recognize your ability to handle these setbacks and continue your pursuit of goals with determination, your confidence in your ability to overcome difficulties increases.
- **Failure helps you expand your comfort zone.** Failure pushes you outside your comfort zone and encourages you to take risks.

By embracing new challenges and learning from unsuccessful attempts, you broaden your experiences and skills.
- **Failure helps you develop problem-solving skills.** Failure often presents complex problems or obstacles that must be overcome. Each failure becomes an opportunity to refine strategies, explore alternative approaches, and develop more effective solutions. As competence in problem solving grows, so does confidence in your ability to tackle future challenges.
- **Failure helps you overcome your fear of failure.** Failure, when viewed as a natural part of the learning process, helps you realize that setbacks are not insurmountable. This shift in mindset cultivates confidence and a growth-oriented attitude toward challenges.

Failure serves as a catalyst for growth, pushing individuals to learn, adapt, and ultimately develop confidence and competence. By embracing failure as an opportunity for learning and improvement, school leaders and their teams can harness its transformative power to propel them toward greater achievement.

Leaders who believe in their staff create psychologically safe environments where educators feel safe and secure enough to make thousands of daily decisions and know it's OK if some are incorrect. When managing challenging student behavior, teachers must know they'll be supported rather than judged. For example, consider a scenario in which a student gets on the wrong bus on the first day of 6th grade after the principal has repeatedly announced that teachers should make sure each student knows how they're going home. In a psychologically safe space, the principal would not berate the teacher by exclaiming, "How did this happen? How did the student get on the wrong bus? Did you check to see how all the students were going home? We announced it four times!" Instead, the principal might ask, "What can we do tomorrow to ensure all students get on the correct bus?"

## Unmasking

One obstacle to developing deeper and more authentic relationships with teachers is when teachers do not feel safe enough to be honest and vulnerable. During Jessica's time as a school-based instructional coach and in her current role as a district-level coach, she is often in classrooms supporting new teachers and coaching all teachers in professional growth. She distinctly remembers spending time in Carrie's language arts class listening to the poem "We Wear the Mask" by Paul Laurence Dunbar, which got her thinking about how people mask feelings and their true selves. The class visit was followed by a mentoring meeting with new teachers and mentors. With the poem and meeting fresh in her mind, Jessica thought about how new teachers and—let's be honest—all of us wear masks while on the job. How can you, as a school leader, help educators remove the masks they wear? Following are ways to approach the most common masks.

### Mask 1: "I'm OK"

If you need to ask someone if they're OK, they are likely not OK. You picked up on some indicator—body language, actions, or words—that made you pause and check in. When leaders ask teachers if they're OK, there's an implication that the other person *should* be OK. Sometimes teachers are not, and that's OK. If staff wear the "I'm OK" mask, they may miss out on support from caring people.

We must help others to remove this mask by normalizing being a human with emotions. The truth is that some days, teachers carry the weight of a personal situation or are processing a difficult day at work. Instead of asking, "Are you OK?" try saying, "Tell me about your day." We've found that inviting conversation helps people reveal more about what they are struggling with than asking a direct question. There are times when questions feel like accusations, which causes the person on the receiving end to become defensive and less likely to be honest.

Moreover, if you have learned that a colleague is dealing with a difficult situation, either personal or professional, it's not helpful to ask if they're OK. Even with the sincerest of intent, it can come across as intrusive or trigger emotions. Instead of leaning into curiosity, try leaning into compassion and offering support by "taking things off their plate" if they're open to acts of service.

## Mask 2: "I'm Good"

When teachers wear the "I'm good" mask, they're shielding themselves from revealing that they need help. This response can also be accompanied by shaking their head side to side or putting their arms up (almost pushing their arms in front to create distance). The "I'm good" response is a deflection. It means the person is not feeling safe and comfortable enough to share their needs. They don't feel like they can ask for help. If someone is truly thriving, their energy and enthusiasm are evident. You probably wouldn't even think to ask them if they are OK because they are open and proactively seeking the resources or support they need. All staff want to feel competent and confident in their work. When they're offered unsolicited help, it can feel like a judgment of their capabilities.

Navigating this situation can be tricky for leaders. Offer to be a thought partner or a collaborative problem solver. Don't assume that your assistance is going to be perceived as helpful. Leverage existing structures to normalize coaching for all teachers, not just "bad" ones. Model vulnerability by asking for help and soliciting feedback from staff to open the door of trust and increase teachers' receptiveness to support. The "I'm good" mask only isolates teachers from the support available to them.

## Mask 3: "I Know"

The "I know" mask or nodding in agreement is a way for staff to avoid acknowledging that they may need to ask questions, seek clarification, or even admit to a lack of knowledge. Dismissing the opportunity to learn something or hear information again is a missed opportunity to affirm or deepen understanding. New information constantly comes to light; whether teachers are new or experienced, no one is expected to know everything about everything. It's important to reinforce the idea that declaring that you don't know is better than trying to pretend that you do.

As a school leader, head off your staff's penchant for donning the "I know" mask by creating an expectation that questions are a part of meetings. For example, end a faculty meeting with each table or group sharing a question with the assembly. Mentors can help new teachers craft questions, or they can co-create a list. Instead of asking individual teachers questions, invite them to tell you about a particular topic or share how a particular action is going. This invitation to share knowledge can reveal misconceptions or incomplete understanding. It can also reveal promising practices or success stories. Share with staff how you build your own understanding by asking questions or conducting further research. Model the value of saying, "I don't have the answer right now, but I'll research it and get back to you" or "I've completed research regarding this topic, and here's what I'm thinking." Demonstrate that knowledge is a perpetual quest and that asking questions is a natural part of the process.

### Mask 4: "I Can"

When leaders invite teachers to take on responsibilities, they may not realize that some teachers feel pressured into saying yes. Invitations should not be expectations. Staff need to remove the "I can" mask to prevent overcommitting or agreeing to a task out of fear or flattery. Before inviting staff to participate in a task, be sure it aligns with the staff member's goals. Expect the possibility of—and gracefully accept—a "no" response. Respect boundaries. Just because someone *can* do something doesn't mean they *should*.

Sometimes, requests repeatedly land on the same person. One person can't do it all, and no one should expect that to be the case. Staff members may be *able* to do a task, but that doesn't mean they have the bandwidth. Prevent burnout by distributing requests across your staff rather than targeting a select few. Don't wrap invitations with guilt or ulterior motives. Instead of asking, "Can you do this for me?" try phrasing the invitation as "Does this opportunity take advantage of your knowledge and skills and feel like an experience that will help you grow?" If the answer is yes, the next question is "Do you have the bandwidth to commit to the opportunity?" And finally, "How can I help you be successful?"

### Mask 5: "I Don't Care"

Staff usually wear the "I don't care" mask to protect hurt feelings, which may be accompanied by deep sighs, eye rolls, or throwing hands up. It's easier for someone to brush off frustration and say "I don't care" than to address the fact that they're having an emotional response. However, opting out only leads to more frustration and resentment. We all care about things that affect us, so pretending that we don't only delays the inevitable reality of dealing with the situation.

When you recognize frustration in your staff, granting space to acknowledge issues and design solutions is essential. Provide opportunities for teachers to submit an issue or problem and spend time thinking about solutions. Then, test the solutions to determine whether they solve the problem or minimize negative effects. Re-engaging teachers wearing the "I don't care" mask is critical to having a cohesive faculty that works toward a common goal. Care about the lack of caring.

## Set an Example

As a leader, you can't expect others to take off their masks if you always wear one. Be aware of the masks you put on as a leader. As mentioned in the beginning of the chapter, Jessica experienced a period of struggling and adjusting to a new school. When she was brave enough to remove her mask, she found that staff members quickly provided support and compassion. In fact, her instructional coach, district-level coaches, and teammates served as valuable thought partners, proposing solutions to help meet her needs. Being vulnerable is a courageous act, and modeling it can feel scary. However, it creates the conditions for others to follow suit. We invite you to remove your own masks and help others remove theirs.

Expectations play a crucial role in employee development. If leaders believe in the potential for growth and improvement, staff will value continuous learning and take on challenges that contribute to their professional growth. High expectations can boost motivation and confidence. When individuals feel that others believe in their abilities, it can enhance their self-esteem, encourage a positive mindset, and lead to increased effort and persistence in the face of challenges. Staff are more likely to stay at a school where they feel valued and believed in.

## Empathy Episode

Read the following Empathy Episode and imagine what it would feel like to be in the teacher's position. Then use the reflection questions to consider leadership blind spots and how to remedy them.

> After several years of effective teaching, you believe your next career step is to become an assistant principal. You've already completed licensure requirements and one leadership development program. When you expressed the desire to move into school leadership, your current principal was unusually silent on the matter, and you wonder why he still hasn't expressed support or encouragement.
>
> In the final few weeks before summer break, you offer to help the principal prepare for the next school year. Your intent is to help with scheduling or planning so that you can expand your skill set while also supporting your principal. The principal responds, "Thanks, but I think we've got it. Enjoy your summer!" However, he does ask you to coach cheerleading, which doesn't give you opportunities to develop the leadership skills necessary to advance your career. You infer that your principal is not willing to help you advance toward a future role as an assistant principal.
>
> While serving as the cheerleading coach, you travel to other schools and chat informally with school leaders and teachers. One leader asks if your principal supports you and shares that your principal said, "It's hard to take [your name] seriously. I just don't see [your name] moving into school leadership." You're in shock for a few minutes, but then the hurt sets in. Whereas you previously questioned whether your principal believed in you, now you know he doesn't.
>
> Feeling demotivated by this realization, you stop investing in the school. You submit your resignation from the cheerleading coach position, and you wake up each day dreading going to work.

### Reflection Questions

- How would the actions of the principal in the scenario be different if he believed in the candidate?
- What impact does the lack of belief and support have on the teacher and consequently on students?

Responding with silence was a missed opportunity for the principal to vocalize his support for the teacher's desire to develop leadership skills and prepare for the next step in her career. Instead, the principal could have replied, "How can I support you in achieving this goal?" Another misstep was dismissing the teacher's offer to help prepare for the next school year. Preparing involves a significant amount of work, so the principal could have reduced his own workload by accepting help. Doing so would also have allowed the teacher to learn leadership skills in an authentic setting. Often staff become more empathetic when they get a glimpse into the amount of work that happens "behind the scenes" of school operations.

In his comments to the other school leader, the principal probably thought he was simply speaking candidly about one of his staff members. If he wished to express support, a better phrasing would have been "I was surprised by her interest in school leadership. I'm trying to think of opportunities to support her growth. Do you have any suggestions?"

In serving as a cheerleading coach, the teacher developed some leadership experience to build from. But her desire to grow was met with rejection, which negatively affects esteem.

## How Will You Commit?

- What strategies from this chapter are you committed to implementing?
- Who can help you implement these strategies?
- What outcome do you want to see as a result of implementing these strategies?

## Summary

In this chapter, we discussed the power of believing in staff members. Believing in staff means knowing their strengths and recognizing that failure is a part of growth and builds confidence and competence. In developing authentic relationships with teachers, it's important to focus on educators' reluctance to express vulnerability. By removing metaphorical masks and encouraging genuine communication, leaders can create an environment where educators feel supported and valued.

Now that the foundation of knowing strengths and working toward achieving goals has been established, the next step is to keep the momentum going. This is the topic we will discuss in Chapter 6.

# 6

# Igniting an Eternal Flame

*Not only did [the assistant principal] prioritize my students' growth when he watched their meteorological presentations, but he also took an opportunity to push me professionally. When we turned in our final paperwork for the grant, which was fully funded, he asked me how I felt. I responded with, "I feel like I'm the teacher I'm supposed to be." That experience helped me see how much potential I had. It set me up for success in my classroom, gave me the confidence to apply for other grants, and challenged me to seek out opportunities to share my work with educators throughout East Tennessee.*

—6th grade science teacher

Most educators enter the profession with a fiery passion, yet, according to the National Center for Education Statistics (Goldring et al., 2014), 8 percent of teachers leave the profession annually. To put that number in perspective, out of a faculty of 50, 4 teachers leave the profession every year. Others may transfer to other schools or transition to different roles, but every year, four decide to leave teaching altogether.

If you've been in education a while, you've known teachers who chose to leave. Maybe you thought, *Good for them!* Or maybe you lamented, *What a loss for students!* Teacher turnover and movement disrupt student learning, destabilize schools, and strain time and resources. Teacher dissatisfaction is real, as is its impact on students, colleagues who stay, and school leaders. One of the reasons we wrote this book is to identify ways you can make your school a better place for students, teachers, and leaders to grow.

This chapter explores how leaders can ignite an eternal flame that inspires effective teachers and sustains them as they ply their craft. To get a sense of how your school is currently doing in this area, take a moment to complete the self-assessment in Figure 6.1.

FIGURE 6.1

**Retaining Staff Self-Assessment**

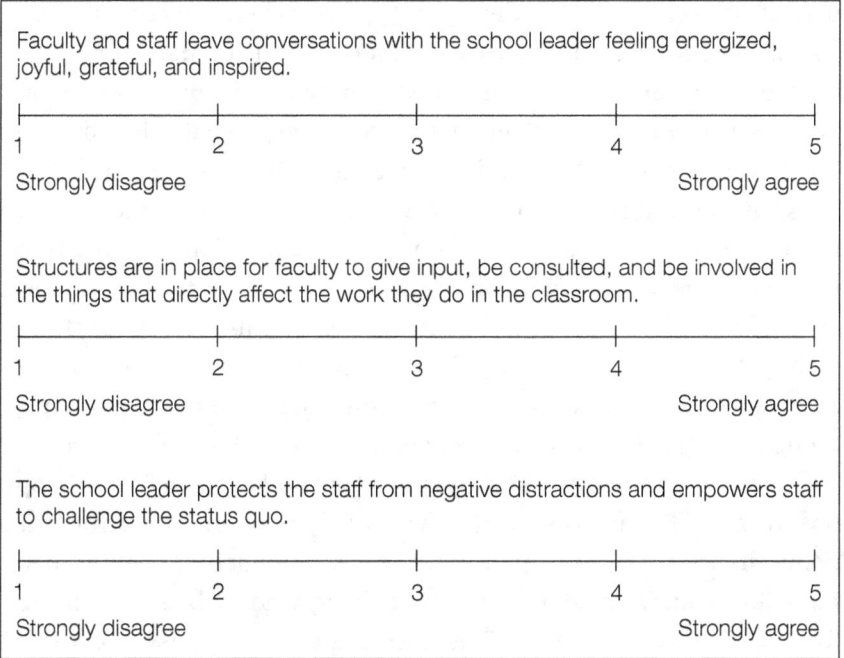

## Culture, Climate, and Lighting the Way

Culture is ubiquitous and can be the most effective retention tool or the final straw for educators. *Workplace culture* refers to the shared values, beliefs, attitudes, and behaviors that characterize the working environment of an organization. It encompasses the norms and unwritten rules that shape how individuals interact, how work is accomplished, and how the school operates. Workplace culture is a powerful force that influences employee attitudes, motivation, and overall organizational success.

In comparison, *workplace climate* refers to atmosphere, mood, and conditions. It's the prevailing "feel" of the work environment and is influenced by factors such as interpersonal relationships, communication, leadership style, and organizational practices. Unlike workplace culture, which is more deeply rooted and enduring, workplace climate can change more quickly and often reflects the current state of affairs within the organization. The climate of a school is often described as the "vibe" or the feeling you get when you're in a school. As coaches, Jessica and Carrie can determine the climate of a particular school after spending just a few minutes in the building. No one has to say a thing; it's written on people's faces, revealed by how they interact with one another, and shown by how they respond to visitors.

Consider taking a mood check as staff enter your school or at the end of a meeting by posting a simple chart of emoji and asking them to place a check mark next to the one that represents their current emotional state. You can also tally smiles to gauge how people are feeling. If you detect an overall increase in dissatisfaction, it's time to elicit feedback and take action. If an individual is frequently unhappy, it might be time for a check-in conversation with that staff member.

People are unlikely to stay in a place that makes them feel unhappy or stressed. If they do stay, they will likely put minimal effort into doing their job. We hear a lot of talk about supporting new teachers; however, leaders must not overlook those who've been on the job for years—maybe decades. These veterans often "pass the torch" by mentoring new teachers and serving in leadership positions. But those who feel overlooked and undervalued may see their passion for the profession dwindle to embers. As a school leader, it's imperative that you be aware of all staff members' feelings about their work and develop a plan for lighting the way forward for each one of them.

## Maintaining the Flame by Knowing the Why and the Goals

To maintain an eternal flame, educators must consistently revisit their "why," which is essential to understanding their purpose, values, and motivations. Revisiting and recommitting to their why is critical for several reasons. As educators, they have many competing priorities claiming to be *the* thing that they should focus on. Initiatives, curricular resources, standards, and students—they all change. At times, it may feel as if everything is written in bold, and it can be challenging to determine what's truly important. The why does not change. It's a constant among all the variables.

Clarity about why they're in the profession and what they want to accomplish can be the inspiration and drive that educators need to overcome the inevitable challenges and changes they face. Ultimately, when their decisions align with their values, they feel more fulfilled and experience greater purpose and satisfaction.

To keep a flame burning, a school leader must notice when things get dim. Sometimes people who are burning out are not vocal or overtly negative. "Quiet quitters" just disengage and continue to do the bare minimum while collecting a paycheck (Klotz & Bolino, 2022). In contrast, at some point, we've all been blindsided by someone who suddenly and unexpectedly left the teaching profession. Although the reasons may be as unique as the educators themselves, one thing unites them all. The why that drew them to the education profession has been extinguished by something else. If we know what that something else is, we can better support and retain teachers.

In *The Infinite Game*, Simon Sinek (2019) says, "Mature companies fail because they forget why they were born" (p. 48). We all understand that the first year of a business is the riskiest and are surprised when a business that has operated for many years suddenly closes. Sinek's maxim explains this phenomenon. Applying the metaphor to veteran educators suggests that leaders would do well to continuously remind those they lead of their why and remove any obstacles to that knowledge. We've seen educators ask themselves, "Why am I doing this?" and not have an answer. That lack of purpose leads to frustration and discontent and often ends in the educator exiting the profession. To ignite and maintain an eternal flame, we must cultivate a culture that keeps purpose at the forefront. Furthermore, although we know how critical the first five years of an educator's professional experiences are, we cannot overlook the importance of the last five. Educators rounding the corner to retirement still deserve to grow and be valued school staff members.

In addition to making sure educators remember their why, structure time for them to define their short-term and long-term goals. Clear objectives can provide a sense of purpose and motivation. Then help them connect their personal goals and objectives with the broader purpose of the school. Recognize how their contributions positively affect others in the school community.

> **Try This: Conscious Goal Monitoring**
>
> Throughout the school year, intentionally plan time for activities that help teachers connect their goals and their personal why to positive outcomes or impact. Use data to show the value of their work. Leverage structures already in place, such as formal observation feedback sessions and midyear conferences, to explicitly identify connections and impact.
>
> Have educators share their why with one another and reflect on how their actions and interactions align with their why. Use the *share, reflect, align, troubleshoot,* and *recall* protocol to have staff name, determine how to act out, and navigate obstacles in staying true to their why.
>
> - **Share**—Have each person take turns sharing their personal reasons—their why—for being an educator. Their why could include values, passions, and the impact they hope to make.
> - **Reflect**—After each sharing session, provide some time for reflection. Encourage others to share their thoughts on what resonated with them from their colleague's why. This can be done through written reflections on sticky notes or chart paper, or through open discussion.
> - **Align**—Facilitate a discussion on how staff members can align their daily actions and interactions with their shared values and purpose. Encourage them to brainstorm specific strategies or changes in practice that would bring them closer to living out their why in the educational setting. Remember, the key is to create a safe and open space to share and support each other in aligning actions with shared purpose.
> - **Troubleshoot**—Ask educators what is getting in the way of their why and how you can remove obstacles. This part of the activity can either be done simultaneously with the initial activity or later. Again, it may be best to have participants write their responses on a sticky note or chart paper. Take the time to co-create solutions and be sure to follow up on whether those solutions are working.

- **Recall**—Have educators think of a teacher, coach, or other school personnel who made a positive difference in their life as a student. Ask them to share with a partner who the person was and what they did to have that impact. As a group, make a chart of these lasting impacts. To conclude the activity, ask participants to reflect on their current role and consider how to pay the positive difference forward: "How can you be like your benefactor?" Post the charts in a community room or shared space, such as a teachers lounge or mailbox area, to showcase the legacy that earlier educators have left for the current staff.

## Bridging Passion and Purpose

During a recent walk in her neighborhood, Carrie ran into an older gentleman, a PE teacher and tennis coach, and asked him, "When are you going to retire?" He quickly replied, "Retire from what?" as his face lit up with a playful smile. After processing his response, Carrie smiled back and said, "Oh. You do love what you do, don't you?" He confirmed, "Yes. My father told me to find something I love, and I'd never work a day in my life. Being an educator is part of who I am, and I won't ever retire from that." As Carrie continued walking, she thought of the man's words. What made him want to keep teaching after 50 years? He always seemed balanced and joyful, and he possessed an infectious enthusiasm. The encounter made Carrie reflect on the power of finding passion and purpose in one's work.

The PE teacher's half-century-plus dedication exemplifies a deep love for his craft. His father's advice to find something he loved had clearly guided his career choice, allowing him to approach each day enthusiastically and joyfully. His commitment to teaching went beyond the job—it became a fundamental part of his identity.

Let's consider the significance of how finding such passion influences an individual's happiness as well as their impact on others. The PE teacher has likely inspired many students to embrace learning, stay active, and develop their own passions. While acknowledging that retirement is a special season in life and this gentleman deserves this time, Carrie couldn't help but appreciate the profound lesson she learned from him—that she was lucky to have found fulfillment in her own work and to have it align with her personal values and passions.

She felt renewed appreciation and true joy for the privilege of serving in her profession. Inspired by the PE teacher's words and demeanor, she vowed to continue pursuing her passions and infusing them into her work, knowing that doing so would lead to a lifetime of purpose and happiness.

What do your staff members love to do? Humans are driven by emotions and passions. Look for opportunities to bridge your staff members' passions and their why. Two of Jessica's favorite things—things she's passionate about—are visiting national parks and reading. When she was a middle school language arts teacher, she found ways to bring both to learning experiences to help her students develop as readers, writers, and thinkers. For example, she wanted them to visualize how many books they had read, so she created a "reading tree" outside the classroom where students added a leaf every time they finished an independent-reading book. The display became both a source of pride and a place where students looked for book recommendations. Jessica also started a reading celebration called Camp Read-a-Lot to promote the joy of reading. Families set up tents outside and provided snacks while students curled up with a blanket or in a sleeping bag and read, just for the sake of reading, for an entire class period. She invited colleagues to join—and they did. These two expressions of Jessica's love of reading brought her much joy as she shared her passion with her students in unique ways.

Educators can also share their personal passions and talents with students through special-interest clubs or workshops. We know of one school where students signed up for teacher-run clubs and workshops on topics that included writing, pottery, art, guitar, learning to change a flat tire, personal fitness, baking, and creating posters for an upcoming football game. One teacher with a passion for crocheting also ran a small business to sell her handmade items, and when students expressed an interest in learning the craft, she established and led a club for them to do so. Gatherings such as these can provide educators with opportunities to interact with students in positive, low-key ways—and they can give students a sense of belonging too.

Knowing what "extracurricular" talents your staff members have can lead to opportunities to leverage those talents and enhance their sense of connection to and appreciation for their work. Another example comes from a teacher who was an accomplished violinist in the local symphony who was invited to play music during a promotion ceremony. Her performance was well received by students, teachers, and families, and she felt appreciated for both her musical talent and her work as an educator.

Inviting school staff to share their passions for the school's overall benefit is obviously worth pursuing, with one caveat: An invitation should not be an expectation. "Volun-telling" a staff member to do something does not make them happy; in fact, it can have the opposite effect on those who are not ready or willing to share their passion with others.

Clearly there's no one-size-fits-all approach to bridging passion and purpose; the possibilities are many, and they're unique to the individuals on your staff. Getting to know your staff as humans, not just educators, will be helpful in building the bridge.

## Tarah's Story

Tarah had been a teacher for a decade, juggling two jobs while seeking to push herself professionally through various fellowships and cohorts. She struggled with the separation between her worlds—her work as a server felt disconnected from her role as an educator. However, this gap began to narrow when she found ways to integrate her passion for food into her teaching. She started small, using edible models to teach about Earth's layers, making butter as the early American colonists did, and baking homemade bread with her students. These activities gradually sparked a transformation in her classroom, capturing the attention of her administrators. "I was starting to see a change in my students," Tarah recalls, "and that's when the idea for Cooking Up Learning was born."

Tarah took an innovative approach to merge her culinary skills with her educational background, creating a unique classroom experience that met her students' basic needs while promoting higher engagement and learning. The turning point came when Tarah presented her idea in a funding competition, seeking financial support from a group of strangers. "I felt like I was on a roller coaster, right at the peak, before the first drop," she remembers. When her name was called as a finalist, everything changed. Not only did she receive initial funding, but her administrators also backed her vision, leading to the remodeling of part of the school's outdated library into a full culinary lab and STEM room. Within a year, Tarah had formed partnerships with nearly 10 community organizations, and the program's momentum seemed unstoppable.

Then COVID-19 hit, and the program's growth came to a sudden halt. Tarah felt defeated as her passion and connections dwindled. She began questioning her future. What if she left the classroom? Could she grow Cooking Up Learning into something bigger? Could she bring her concept to other schools, perhaps with a food truck? These questions haunted her, but she kept them to herself.

Just as hope seemed dim, Tarah learned about a new, permanent position at a local elementary school—a role designed specifically for culinary integration that aligned perfectly with her vision for Cooking Up Learning. "It felt unreal," she says. "I was like a phoenix rising from the ashes, reborn and full of excitement for the future." The opportunity reignited her passion, transforming her from a defeated educator into one who was ready to embrace a future full of promise and potential.

Tarah's story illustrates how infusing personal and professional passions can reignite the flame of a teacher's dedication to education. On the brink of leaving the profession, she instead rekindled her joy in teaching by bringing culinary education into her social studies class. Tarah is not only enjoying teaching again but also lighting the way for others to integrate culinary components into their instruction.

## Encouraging Input and Influence

Having a voice in decision making makes educators feel valued by school leadership. Not having a voice leads to disengagement, frustration, and low morale. Including the voice of only a few creates resentment and allows some to opt out or deflect responsibility because they "did not make that decision."

We developed a Diversity/Inclusivity Matrix (see Figure 6.2) to categorize the advantages and disadvantages to teams with varying degrees of diversity and inclusivity. Each quadrant of the matrix has bullet points that describe four characteristics for each type of team: the nature of decision making, team dynamics, equity, and overall feelings.

FIGURE 6.2

**Diversity/Inclusivity Matrix**

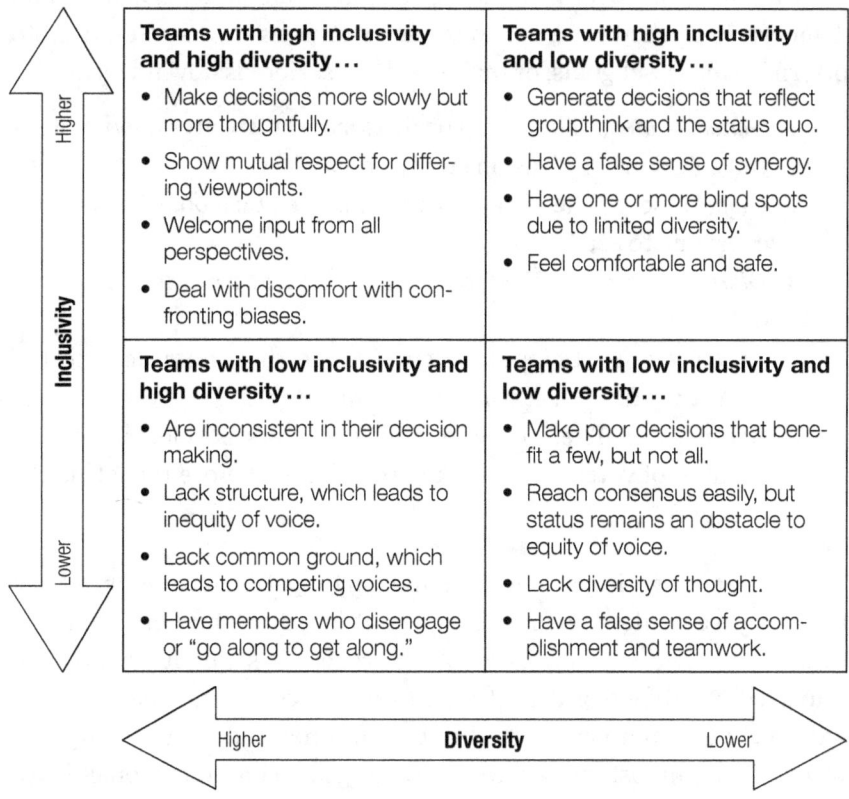

Although high inclusivity and high diversity are the ideal components for team decision making, it's essential to acknowledge that reaching a consensus within that combination can be both challenging and time-consuming. For example, Jessica coached a principal through updating the school's mission and vision to include an emphasis on STEM education. Representation on the teams making decisions mattered because the results would affect everyone. The inclusivity factor was addressed by including a staff member from each grade level and elective. To achieve a high level of diversity, the principal and Jessica selected some staff who were invested in STEM education and others who were skeptical to engage in critical conversations about envisioning the school's future. Using decision-making protocols helped to mitigate the potential challenges of coming to a consensus.

One such protocol is sticker dot voting—a simple, efficient, and democratic method for a group to reach consensus. It's often used to prioritize ideas, set goals, or make decisions. Here is how it works:

1. *Generate ideas.* The group brainstorms and writes down potential solutions or ideas on sticky notes.
2. *Display ideas.* The sticky notes are posted on a board or wall for everyone to see.
3. *Distribute stickers.* Each participant is given a number of sticker dots.
4. *Cast votes.* Participants silently place their dots next to the ideas they find most valuable or important.
5. *Count votes.* The idea with the most dots is selected (or the number of votes is used to narrow the list before repeating the process).

Sticker dot voting promotes equal participation; everyone gets an equal say, regardless of their position. It is a quick and efficient way to narrow down options. The voting process is straightforward and unbiased. As they work together to reach a consensus, participants will likely feel more connected to one another and to the group as a whole. This can foster a sense of belonging and shared responsibility.

> **Try This: Recognize Success**
>
> Staff recognition is vital to maintaining the flame. Good intentions aren't enough; a school leader should consciously attend to recognizing *all* staff to avoid negative unintended consequences. Lack of recognition can be demoralizing for those who feel excluded. Here are some ways to acknowledge your staff's contributions:

- *Create a reporting system for staff to recognize themselves or colleagues.* A digital form such as Google Forms or SurveyMonkey is an efficient way to collect recognition requests. Make the recognition public via a monthly newsletter, as a welcoming ritual at meetings, or in a display in the building's common areas.
- *Establish a straightforward procedure for nominating Teacher of the Year.* This form of recognition can become a popularity contest and cause resentment among staff if the nomination process lacks clarity or transparency.
- *Share success stories about the differences educators are making in students' lives.* For example, recognize the teachers who contributed to the growth of a student who advanced two levels on a recent assessment, or a teacher who always picks up trash, leading a parent to report that their child has started to do the same.
- *Create a "brag board" where you post positive comments from parents, community members, district personnel, and others.*
- *Follow a consistent plan to acknowledge birthdays, baby showers, retirements, and other occasions.*
- *Recognize veterans on Veterans Day.*
- *Show regular appreciation for all staff.* Share personalized notes of appreciation, gratitude, and encouragement frequently. Hold an annual cookout or collective event during which administrators serve staff in some capacity.
- *Be generous with verbal expressions of appreciation.* "Thank you" goes a long way in positively affecting school culture and relationships with staff.

# Rekindling the Flame

Sometimes an educator feels disenchanted or consistently frustrated because they've hit a dead end in their growth journey. Following are some ideas for how to help someone overcome this state of mind.

## Co-Creating a New Path

One way to help burned-out educators is by co-creating a new path with them. This is not a patch to fill the potholes in the road—there's a big difference between fixing a problem and creating a solution. A new path focuses not on what we *don't* want but rather on what we *do* want. It is a route that is intentionally created, fresh, new, and real.

Co-creating a new path might mean approaching the teacher about a different teaching assignment or helping them find a different role within the school or district. It honors the educator's ability to contribute while also helping to create and clear a path for them. The process often starts by helping an educator adjust their mindset about their career and then develop or expand a skill set. School leaders can support staff by encouraging them to engage with professional communities, attend professional learning events, and connect with individuals with related positions. Networking can not only provide support during the transition to a new role but also create opportunities for collaboration.

## Encouraging Innovation

It's common for educators to feel discontent after several years in the profession. Innovation is one way to dispel this malaise. Just because a teacher has always taught a lesson or unit a certain way doesn't mean they should continue to do so. Plenty of projects and lessons are part of the curriculum because they're traditional or because it's easier to use them than to "reinvent the wheel." Help your staff renew their fire by encouraging them to consider redesigning learning experiences by incorporating elements such as learning expeditions, guest speakers, career connections, project-based learning, or new technology tools. They may also rethink the design of their learning space by painting walls, getting new seating or furniture, arranging desks and tables in a new way, or increasing the functionality of wall space.

## Investing in Others

Another way to help educators get out of a funk is to encourage their investment in others. This might mean asking a veteran educator to mentor newer staff or inviting a teacher who has many best practices to share to facilitate professional learning for their peers. Passing on one's own expertise automatically shifts a person's focus toward others. Psychologists have long known that giving back and helping others increases happiness. In fact, studies show that giving is associated with lower blood pressure and stress, less depression, and higher self-esteem (Snyder, 2020).

## Extinguishing a Bonfire of Negativity

School leaders can't light the way for others if their light is overtaken by the flames radiating from a bonfire of negativity. As a leader, it's important to extinguish such bonfires and check regularly to ensure no smoldering embers are waiting to reignite. Doing so requires understanding the root cause of the negativity, which may relate to unmet needs or unperceived problems. Unfortunately, negativity spreads like wildfire and can quickly affect those who are new to the profession or the school. Sometimes, proverbial smoke is seen before the fire in the form of parking lot conversations, eye rolls, lip biting, or defensive body language. It can sound like gossip, complaining, or defiance. More than likely, some people will warn you of existing negativity. Listen to these human smoke alarms, and act as quickly as possible. The worst option is to make dismissive statements such as "I can't make everyone happy" or avoidance statements such as "They'll get over it eventually."

Remember that the answer to negativity is *not* what is sometimes called "toxic positivity." Being disingenuously upbeat leads to unrealistic expectations and the bottling up of other emotions. Toxic positivity is a mask that denies people the ability to feel the range of human emotions and forces them to project a positive exterior while ignoring their needs and emotions. It will lead to resentment, frustration, and divisiveness.

Striking a balance between addressing concerns and maintaining a positive environment is crucial. When Carrie served as an instructional coach, a teacher came to her office to express frustration about students cheating on a test. Instead of dismissing the concerns or jumping straight into problem solving, Carrie acknowledged the teacher's feelings and validated his experience. She said, "I understand that dealing with students cheating can be really irritating, and it's completely normal to be upset about it." Then she encouraged an open dialogue by asking for more details. She asked, "So which students told you about the answer sharing and cheating?" This question allowed the teacher to vent and gave Carrie a deeper understanding of the issue at hand. She learned that the teacher felt disrespected. He also said he was initially overjoyed with the high scores, only to feel foolish when some students revealed the cheating. Now he felt that the scores came from cheating rather than highly effective teaching. Carrie understood the significance of this disappointment, so she looked more deeply into the data and realized that many students who did not cheat had indeed showed tremendous growth. She shared the information with the teacher, who was pleased to hear his instruction did result in increased learning.

After discussing upcoming challenges, Carrie helped the teacher transition into a solution-oriented mindset. Instead of offering generic positive affirmations, Carrie focused on actionable steps and strategies to address the issue. For instance, she pointed out that accusing students of cheating on this online test but being unable to prove it might hurt his relationship with students; it also could cause students to quit trying if they felt that high scores would lead to accusations of cheating. Carrie asked the teacher to consider another approach: acknowledging that now he knew what the students were capable of and could believe in them. In addition, Carrie noted that the cheating had not involved students purposely looking up answers but rather learning the correct answer due to a technology setting the teacher had inadvertently enabled.

In the end, the teacher chose not to accuse students of cheating and decided instead to emphasize his increased expectations for them going forward. Guess what happened? The students continued to perform at a high level, and on the state test, they achieved the highest scores in the history of their school—and higher than all the other schools in the district.

Toxic positivity would not have helped the teacher process this experience. He needed to get his feelings out, and sharing them with Carrie was much better than unleashing on his students. Carrie's approach acknowledged and validated the teacher's concerns without perpetuating negativity. Her method encouraged a constructive and collaborative mindset, fostering a sense of support and partnership in addressing challenges. The results benefited both the teacher and his students.

People's first reaction to negativity is often a flight response. Sometimes the best strategy for dealing with this response is to engage in one-on-one conversations that acknowledge those feelings and encourage the person to stay curious rather than get defensive.

> **Try This: Collaborative Problem Solving**
>
> If negativity is rearing its head in your school, tackle it with collaborative problem solving. Pulling together people to address the challenges that they are disgruntled about and leading them through the design thinking process to develop solutions, rather than solving problems executively, creates a scenario where people are more invested. Design thinking can empower staff to identify and solve problems that are contributing to negativity. Here are the steps to follow:
>
> - *Empathize.* Who needs what? Why is it important to meet this need? If time permits, conduct empathy interviews by asking open-ended questions to get a sense of a problem or need. For example, you might say, "Tell me about a time when you felt successful at work or school" or "Describe what a successful _____ might look like." Get the perspective of all stakeholders involved in the issue. If possible, observe the issue in action.
> - *Define.* Develop a clear problem statement based on the data collected during the empathize stage. Analyze and synthesize information to be specific in determining who needs what and why it matters.
> - *Ideate.* Generate ideas for solutions without judgment. That means saying "yes and" as collective brainstorming happens. The moment the word "no" or doubt enters this process, creativity ends, which might prevent the best idea from being shared. Out-of-the-box thinking happens when individuals feel safe to share.
> - *Create a prototype.* Filter the ideas by asking, "What's viable? What's feasible? What would be most desirable for the person or persons affected?" Develop a solution prototype by sketching, creating a digital design, or building a model.
> - *Test.* Implement a prototyped solution to determine its effectiveness. Gather data and feedback on the solution. Design thinking is iterative; if the solution isn't ideal, return to defining the problem or prototyping based on data analysis and feedback.
>
> Designing solutions *for* others often misses the mark because the problem is approached from the school leader's perspective. Designing solutions *with* others ensures that the issue is understood, the problem is clearly defined, and staff are empowered to create and test solutions.

> **Try This: Countering Negativity**
>
> Seasons of negativity are inevitable, so rather than waiting for them to arise, try using some of the following proactive strategies to head them off:

- *Meet one-on-one with the teacher and openly discuss concerns.* Listen to understand. Make a plan for how this teacher can speak directly with you about any future concerns. Establish regular feedback channels for teachers, parents, and students to communicate with you. Embrace a culture of continuous improvement.
- *Normalize struggle and frustration.* Lead by example! Demonstrate the behavior and attitude you expect from others. Show resilience, optimism, vulnerability, and a willingness to tackle challenges. Explain how to identify the underlying issue and how it resulted in certain emotions or actions. Then model how to address the underlying issue. Be specific.
- *Show that you value the contributions of teachers and staff.* Acknowledge your staff in the various ways we've described earlier, such as celebrations of their accomplishments or simply remembering to say, "Thank you." Do not assume that teachers and staff know that you appreciate them. Even if they do, they need to hear it. Gestures of appreciation can boost morale and uplift everyone.
- *Establish a code of conduct.* Clearly outline expectations for professional conduct and respectful communication.

## Protecting the Flame

Any career will have peaks and valleys; leaders should be intentional about not contributing to their staff's valleys. To avoid educator fatigue, distribute your "asks" fairly. There always seems to be a core group of staff who get all the requests to take on tasks, while others get by with doing little to nothing. In addition to the risk of fatigue, relying too heavily on a few staff members will result in a big gap in support if they leave or retire.

Rewarding teachers for a job well done with more work is one way to lose staff. Teachers with strong classroom management skills should not be asked to take on more students with behavioral challenges. Rather, they should be invited to share effective practices with their colleagues. Teachers with a track record of increasing student growth should not be assigned more students experiencing academic challenges; they should be encouraged to share their expertise. Overreliance on a few people sends an indirect message to others that you don't believe in them or don't care to invest in their growth. Hold high expectations for all while also supporting and investing in all.

Protecting the flame of educators' dedication to their work requires a strong commitment from leaders. A country song by Mickey

Guyton called "How You Love Someone" (2022) asks if someone's love is "a matchstick minute or forever burning like the Sun." Take a moment to reflect. Is your commitment to education a "matchstick minute"? Or is it "forever burning like the Sun"? Be honest with yourself. Your team is watching to see if you still find the work worthy of your time and talents. You are the keeper of the flame. Are you protecting that flame for others? Four actions can help in this effort: (1) leading by example, (2) inviting input and influence, (3) showing gratitude and appreciation, and (4) investing in relationships.

## Leading by Example

The power of leading by example comes from the message it conveys—namely, that the leader is not above the work. Leaders who actively engage in day-to-day tasks alongside educators cultivate a sense of camaraderie and shared purpose. They not only earn the respect of their team but also create a collaborative spirit that fuels the eternal flame for the whole team. The message is clear: Everyone is an integral part of the educational journey, and no task is beneath anyone.

## Inviting Input and Influence

Protecting a flame requires more than directive leadership; it needs collective input to thrive. As noted earlier, leaders who create avenues for faculty input and influence tap into a wellspring of diverse perspectives and experiences, not only empowering educators but also fostering a sense of ownership. When educators see their ideas having positive effects on students, the eternal flame is kept alive through the collective vision and shared commitment to excellence.

## Showing Gratitude and Appreciation

Gratitude is the fuel that sustains an eternal flame. Our earlier observations in this chapter confirm that leaders who express genuine appreciation for the hard work and dedication of educators create a positive and affirming environment. Recognizing and acknowledging the efforts of each team member not only boosts morale but also reinforces the motivation to make a positive difference, which is what drives most educators.

### Investing in Relationships

The heart of education lies in the relationships forged within the school community. Leaders who prioritize building strong and meaningful connections create an environment of trust, collaboration, and support. Positive relationships among educators, students, and administrators foster a sense of belonging and shared mission. They become the bedrock that enables individuals to endure the challenges of the educational journey.

## Empathy Episode

Read the following Empathy Episode and imagine what it would feel like to be in the teacher's position. Then use the reflection questions to consider leadership blind spots and how to remedy them.

> It's your first year at a new school, but your 15th year of teaching. Despite being told in the interview that your wealth of instructional experience and innovative ideas would be welcome additions to the school community, you're never given the opportunity to share your insights or contribute to decision-making processes.
>
> After a few weeks, you realize that most staff have worked at the school for 10 years or more. Some even attended as students or have children who are current students. You feel like an outsider. Your input is rarely sought, and your efforts in the classroom go unnoticed. In staff meetings, you sit quietly while the principal and other teachers discuss curriculum changes, school initiatives, and instructional strategies. The same few teachers always speak up during meetings and leave little opportunity for anyone else to share ideas. There seems to be no structure or process for providing input, and you fear that speaking up would be viewed as interrupting the conversation. You feel as though your voice is not wanted. Self-doubt creeps in. You wonder, "Does my voice matter?"
>
> You begin to understand how and why people become "quiet quitters" as you silently disengage from the very profession you once loved. Lacking opportunities to provide input and feeling undervalued take a toll on your morale. You start to question your abilities and whether your contributions are truly making a difference in students' lives. You feel so defeated that you begin calling in sick and taking mental health days once a week.

## Reflection Questions
- How could the school leader in the scenario have ensured that the teacher had input and felt valued?
- What structures could be put in place in meetings to support equity of voice among teachers?

Knowing that most of the staff have worked together for a long period of time, the leader in the scenario could have anticipated that the new hire might feel like an outsider. To forestall this, the leader could have held conversations with existing staff about how to bring others into the group and provide space for new voices. One way to do so would be to structure conversations to promote inclusivity and equity of voice by implementing protocols during staff meetings. For example, the Go-Round Protocol is a simple and effective method for ensuring that every member of a group has an opportunity to speak and contribute to the conversation. It's particularly useful in meetings or discussions where the goal is to gather input from all participants or to ensure that quieter voices are heard. The protocol proceeds as follows:

1. *Introduce the topic.* The facilitator introduces a specific question, topic, or issue that the group needs to discuss. The topic should be clear and concise to ensure everyone understands what they are expected to comment on.
2. *Respond using a structured speaking order.* The facilitator initiates a "go-round," during which each participant is invited to share their thoughts one by one. Participants can either speak in a predetermined order (e.g., clockwise around the room) or voluntarily in the order they feel comfortable. However, it is often most effective to have a set order to avoid confusion and ensure that everyone gets a turn.
3. *Set time limits.* To keep the process efficient, the facilitator may set a time limit for each person's contribution (e.g., one to two minutes per person). This ensures that everyone has a fair opportunity to speak without the discussion running too long.
4. *Observe a "no interruptions" rule.* During the go-round, participants are not allowed to interrupt or respond to others'

comments until everyone has had their turn. This rule helps create a safe space where people can share their thoughts without fear of immediate criticism or debate.
5. *Engage in open discussion (optional).* After everyone has had their turn, the facilitator can open the floor for a more general discussion in which participants can respond to one another's points, ask questions, or elaborate on their own ideas.
6. *Reflect and summarize.* The facilitator may conclude the go-round with a brief reflection or summary, highlighting key points raised during the discussion and identifying any actions or decisions that need to be taken.

Awareness is key to recognizing isolation and disengagement in another person. An increase in absences or decrease in engagement is a signal that you may need to check in with your staff member. Such awareness is closely tied to another kind of awareness—awareness of the need for esteem. One of the five categories in Maslow's hierarchy of needs, esteem involves feeling valued and recognized for one's contributions. Igniting an eternal flame for educators involves creating a culture where their efforts are acknowledged and appreciated. Regular expressions of gratitude and recognition for their dedication can boost morale and motivation. A positive work environment, characterized by trust, collaboration, and respect, supports educators' esteem needs. When educators feel they're part of a supportive community that values their input and expertise, their perception fosters a sense of pride and belonging that, in turn, contributes to the longevity of their passion.

Igniting an eternal flame also aligns closely with the concept of self-actualization. Self-actualized individuals are driven by intrinsic motivation, a deep internal desire to fulfill their potential. Similarly, educators who tap into their passion for teaching and a genuine love of learning are more likely to sustain their enthusiasm over the long term. Self-actualization involves a commitment to ongoing personal and professional development. Educators who embrace a mindset of continuous learning, exploring new teaching methods and staying updated on educational trends, are more likely to keep their flame burning bright. Self-actualized individuals seek meaningful connections and relationships. For educators, building strong connections with students, colleagues, and the broader community provides a sense of purpose and contributes to the lasting impact of their work. Educators, by nature, have the opportunity to contribute significantly to the growth and development of their students, fostering a sense of purpose that can keep their flame burning brightly throughout their careers. When you, as a school leader, encourage educators to pursue self-actualization, you're not only promoting their personal fulfillment but also creating the conditions for them to kindle and sustain an eternal flame of passion, purpose, and impact in their role as educators.

## How Will You Commit?

- What strategies from this chapter are you committed to implementing?
- Who can help you implement these strategies?
- What outcome do you want to see as a result of implementing these strategies?

## Summary

In this chapter, we discussed the transformative leadership practices that contribute to a thriving and energized school community—how to ignite, maintain, protect, and rekindle the flame of passion for education. By establishing robust structures for faculty input and involvement, leaders can create an environment where faculty and staff leave conversations feeling not only heard but also energized, joyful, grateful, and inspired.

A pivotal aspect of positive leadership is protecting staff from negative distractions. Effective school leaders act as shields, ensuring that the faculty's focus remains on the core mission of education and positive outcomes for students. Effective leaders encourage a culture of innovation and continuous improvement, one where faculty members feel empowered to drive positive change within the school community and a shared commitment to excellence. How to build the capacity of educators is the topic we will discuss in Chapter 7.

# 7

# Building Capacity

*I knew that my former administrators trusted my professional judgment and work with colleagues when I was asked to be a grade team leader. They saw my potential to do well in leadership roles when they continued to ask me to work with other school leadership teams. I had opportunities to develop within our school parameters and also felt that, when I was ready to reach out beyond the school walls, I would—and I did.*

—Tammy Musiowsky-Borneman,
professional learning facilitator and coach

Leading alone is not a sustainable model. One principal cannot serve in all leadership roles within a school. Therefore, it's imperative to support others to develop leadership capacities and provide them with opportunities to serve in leadership roles.

Are you investing in the growth of your team? Are you building capacity or dependency? Every staff member contributes to the school's mission and vision; thus, every staff member is a potential leader. Providing your staff with opportunities to expand their skill sets and knowledge will motivate them to reinvest that new expertise into their classrooms and the school. Moreover, they are more likely to become brand ambassadors for your school when they move forward in their careers.

A quote from Episode 12 of the television series *Ted Lasso*, titled "Inverting the Pyramid of Success," captures the essence of leadership development (Lowney et al., 2021). Speaking to a younger colleague, Director of Football Operations Leslie Higgins says, "A good mentor hopes you will move on. A great mentor knows you will." This quote highlights the difference between good and great mentors in their approach to supporting and nurturing individuals' growth. In reality, the school leader is a mentor to everyone on staff. What distinguishes a good mentor from a great one is a great mentor goes beyond hoping for the mentee's progress; they have a deep understanding and belief in the mentee's capabilities. Many who end up in leadership roles have benefited from a great mentor and understand how that person helped them reach their fullest potential. Now it's time to pay it forward.

This chapter explores how to inspire and develop others as leaders. Before proceeding, complete the self-assessment in Figure 7.1 to get a sense of where you and your school stand with regard to building capacity.

## Developing a Leadership Ecosystem

In earlier coal mining days—before the existence of the Occupational Safety and Health Administration—canaries were carried into the mines as an early warning system to detect carbon monoxide and other dangerous gases. If the bird passed out, miners knew that conditions were unsafe for them as well.

As a school leader, what factors serve as your metaphorical canary? What indicators do you have that leaders are being built and developed under your leadership? Are you struggling because there are no other leaders in the school? Is no one stepping up? Do people avoid responsibility? Are they hiding to survive? Are they fearful because of what they've seen others experience?

Leadership is not a position for a single person, and leadership within a school should not be limited to the principal and assistant principal. One sign of a strong leader is the practice of elevating others to leadership roles—a leadership ecosystem within the school. An ecosystem is an interconnected network of organisms and their physical environment. A thriving leadership ecosystem meets the needs of both formal and informal leaders and is characterized by a variety of leadership roles, mentoring and support, and reciprocal benefits. Moreover, the school environment creates conditions for leadership growth and development that benefit the school community as a whole, not just individuals.

FIGURE 7.1

**Building Capacity Self-Assessment**

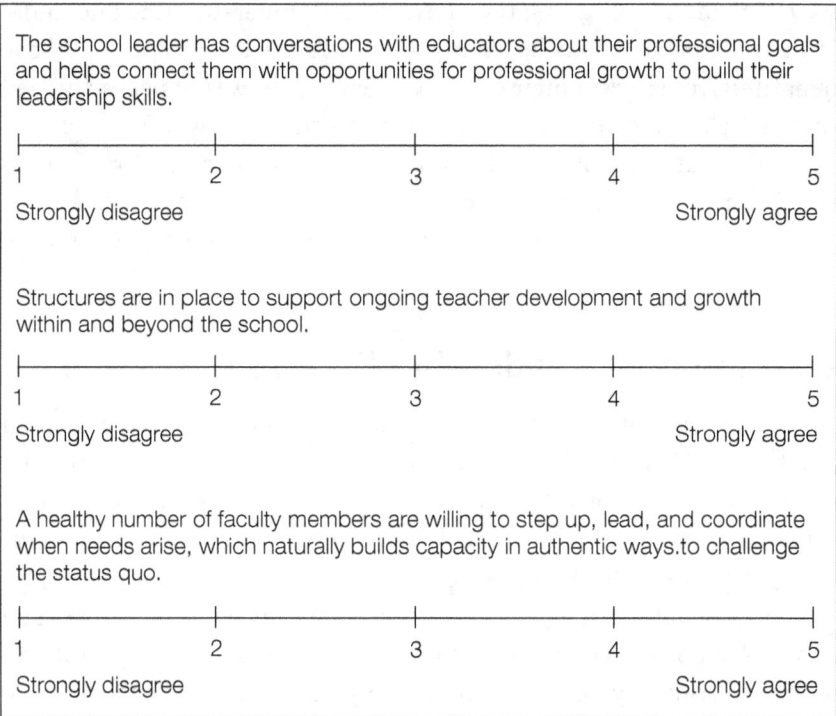

*Servant leaders* are leaders whose priorities focus on others for the betterment of the organization or community. In schools, servant leaders' foremost commitment is to the growth and advancement of each educator under their guidance. This is no easy task, considering many school principals oversee 50 or more direct reports and a building of hundreds or even thousands of students. As daunting and even idealistic as it might sound, by meticulously identifying the pivotal next step for each individual, a school leader can pave a personalized pathway toward elevating that person's pedagogical prowess and overall practice. The goal is to empower educators with tailored support, be it through specialized training programs or by cultivating innovative teaching methods. Concurrently, leaders should support teachers in pursuing leadership roles that align with teachers' strengths and aspirations. Whether it involves developing curriculum and content, engaging in departmental leadership, or participating in schoolwide initiatives, school leaders should wholeheartedly encourage educators to embrace opportunities that amplify their impact and contribute to the collective growth of the educational community. Through this dual commitment to tailored growth and leadership development, school leaders can nurture a dynamic and flourishing ecosystem of teaching excellence.

Recognizing and hiring top educator talent is just the first step in building a successful educational team. Although identifying skilled individuals is crucial, it's equally important to invest in their ongoing development and provide the necessary support structures. High-performing educators are driven by a passion for growth and impact; they want to contribute meaningfully to their students and continue honing their skills.

One of Carrie's experiences as an instructional coach echoes this sentiment. Newly hired at a school, she was excited by the prospect of using her leadership skills to make a difference in students' lives, but her enthusiasm turned into frustration when the promised structures and support were lacking. After multiple conversations with school leaders failed to resolve the issues, she eventually left the school and the field of instructional coaching altogether.

Carrie's experience highlights elements crucial to leadership development that are often lacking in educational settings. Her initial excitement was met with the stark reality of unfulfilled promises and inadequate support structures. The absence of clear expectations communicated to teachers regarding their collaboration with an instructional coach became a significant roadblock. In a school where all teachers operated independently, without collaborative planning, there was a pervasive sentiment that time spent with the instructional coach intruded on precious planning time. The absence of established structures for regular professional development or professional learning communities left the instructional coaching role misunderstood by teachers, creating a barrier to their receptiveness and thwarting Carrie's ability to develop as a school leader.

Hiring an individual based on their existing skills alone is not enough; a commitment to fostering their continuous growth as an educator and leader is essential. A culture of professional development includes offering opportunities for skill enhancement, providing mentorship, and establishing a framework for collaboration. When educators feel supported and empowered, they can channel their skills effectively, benefiting not only their own professional growth but also the overall success of the school.

Being a leader who builds the capacity of others increases the overall impact of leadership. Building capacity is an indicator of a healthy leadership ecosystem, in which achieving collective goals is more important than individual accolades. Underutilizing staff communicates a lack of belief in their current skills or their capacity to acquire skills. Neither of those beliefs sends a positive message. Believe in your staff. Build capacity. Grow leaders.

In our school district, we've witnessed the legacy of growth and development nurtured by a leader who was an administrator at multiple schools and a principal coach during her career. Before meeting her, Jessica had heard positive testimonials about this school leader's impact on teacher growth. Teachers shared stories about how she would cheer for them, have high expectations but also show high levels of support, invest in their professional learning, and build their leadership capacity. When Jessica worked directly with the leader, she witnessed and experienced this capacity building and support firsthand, and it was clear that the educators who had benefited from the leader's guidance would happily work for her again. Leaders who grow more leaders are more likely to attract and keep educators, even in hard-to-staff schools. Capacity builders like Jessica's colleague have made a commitment to the long term, knowing that the connections and capacity they develop in others will enhance their professional expertise beyond the time of working in the same building.

## Leading from the Classroom

For classroom teachers to experience self-actualization, they need avenues to grow and maximize their potential. In the past, the career trajectory for teachers often led to administrative roles such as assistant principal, principal, or a district-level position. However, as the field of education evolves, a wide variety of leadership paths have become available, including roles that allow teachers to stay in the classroom. There's nothing wrong with teachers wanting to continue working directly with students—schools need dedicated educators who find joy and fulfillment in the classroom! Those who prefer student-facing roles are excellent candidates to be teacher leaders. No one should have to leave or change positions to grow their leadership skills.

Serving on school committees is an obvious starting point for teachers to develop leadership skills within the classroom. To provide support, school leaders should focus on building capacity, not dependency. Alissa Farias, an assistant principal, shares her approach: "Every staff member is on a committee, asked to take a role (e.g., recorder or timekeeper) and follow some actionable steps. For instance, our family engagement committee arranges activities throughout the year. Staff lead this work, and the administration supports it." Committees work best when they have a clear focus and goals, such as developing and monitoring a particular component of a school's action plan or overseeing faculty events, family engagement opportunities, and relationships with community partners. Teachers can also lead by serving on district committees where they can represent their school, update colleagues on district-level meetings, collaborate with other educators, and participate in district-level decision-making processes.

Classroom teachers can also model lessons for colleagues and engage in learning labs. Demonstrating effective teaching techniques for other educators is an avenue for teacher leaders based in the classroom to have a broader impact on the school community.

In professional learning communities (PLCs), teachers collaborate to analyze data and improve instruction and outcomes for all students. A teacher can serve as a facilitator for a PLC while still providing daily classroom instruction. Teacher leaders can encourage sharing best practices, insights, and challenges by fostering a collaborative environment within the PLC, enhancing the group's expertise and creating a supportive network where educators can collectively tackle issues and brainstorm innovative solutions. Classroom teachers often have more credibility with their colleagues than educators based outside the classroom, and they're in the best position to understand what will work. In this leadership role, the classroom teacher becomes a catalyst for positive change, influencing both their own students and their fellow educators' growth and development. In addition, they have the opportunity to develop their skill set in facilitating adult learning, which builds their capacity and prepares them to move into other leadership roles, such as instructional coaching, if they choose to. Serving the dual roles of teacher and facilitator makes the PLC a dynamic space for continuous improvement in teaching methodologies and student achievement.

Many fellowship opportunities are available for classroom teachers. By participating in specialized programs or fellowships to gain expertise in a specific area of education, they can grow their skills and bring back new ideas and learning to share with colleagues. For example, when Jessica was selected for a STEM education fellowship, she attended workshops and brought back valuable tools and learning, ultimately leading the school she was serving to earn designation as a STEM school.

Classroom teachers can also take the lead to organize special school events such as STEM nights, exhibit nights, student-led conferences, or other occasions that showcase student work and engage parents and the community. These events allow teacher leaders to grow and expand their skills, elevate promising practices, and celebrate the joy of student learning.

In essence, teacher leadership involves taking on various roles and responsibilities to support the growth and development of both students and colleagues while actively contributing to the improvement of the educational community. It includes collaboration, innovation, advocacy, and a commitment to continuous improvement while engaging with peers and students to foster a positive learning environment.

## Try This: Targeted Peer Observations

Invite teachers to spend some of their planning time visiting two or three of their peers' classrooms for about 10 minutes each. To get maximum benefit from the visits, align them with a current instructional focus. For example, if the school has been focused on the instructional practice of strategic questions, work with teachers to create an observation tool to record the strategic questions they hear during their 10-minute observation and to describe what the practice looks like and sounds like. Include success criteria so that all teachers use the same descriptors. (See below for a template for this kind of tool; two examples of completed observation tools can be found in the Appendix.) Afterward, debrief the observations by discussing what the impact of the selected instructional practice was on student learning. This activity is a powerful form of professional development that can help demystify an instructional practice. To follow up, consider having teachers set a goal for themselves around this instructional practice, and if your building has an instructional coach, have that person work with teachers to provide coaching and support around the goal.

**Instructions:** Use this tool to observe and reflect on the use of *[targeted instructional practice]* during a lesson. Your goal is to identify specific examples of how the teacher's implementation of the practice supports student learning.

**What does *[targeted instructional practice]*...**

| Look like? | Sound like? |
|---|---|
|  |  |

| **Reflection:** |
|---|
| When *[teacher name] [took specific action], [describe benefits for student learning]*. |

| **Success criteria (identify at least three qualities of successful implementation):** |
|---|
| • |
| • |
| • |

## Leading Within the School

District leader Molly Plyer explains her approach to building leadership capacity this way:

> I look at body language and try to hear the words the staff are telling me. While it's tempting to ask the "rock stars" to lead all the things, it is important to build capacity among staff and allow each person opportunities to step back and experience restorative moments.

Leadership opportunities with broader responsibilities within a school can take a variety of forms. Many schools appoint chairpersons to lead and coordinate the activities of a specific academic department, such as language arts or math. Teachers may have the opportunity to lead grade-level teams, with responsibilities that include facilitating collaborative planning, sharing resources and best practices, and coordinating curriculum implementation within the team. Most schools employ instructional coaches who support and guide teachers in improving their instructional practices. These coaches often have leadership responsibilities in mentoring and teacher development, modeling effective teaching techniques, and facilitating professional development. Teachers may also be involved in writing curriculum guides or providing guidance around effective implementation of high-quality instructional materials.

Another opportunity for in-school leadership comes in the form of a *multiclassroom leader* (MCL). Teachers in this role engage in collaborative coaching and work closely with two or three teachers who teach the same content or grade, offering one-on-one coaching and mentoring to help them improve their teaching practices. MCLs facilitate data analysis with their team. Together, they analyze student performance data to identify areas of improvement and develop targeted strategies. MCLs also help colleagues develop resources such as instructional materials and lesson plans, organize and facilitate sessions or workshops to enhance their peers' teaching skills, conduct classroom observations, and provide constructive feedback. They actively contribute to school leadership team meetings, sharing insights and representing the interests of their teacher group. Finally,

MCLs advocate for changes or improvements in curriculum, assessment, or school policies for the benefit of both teachers and students.

Building leadership capacity in members of your school community is a critical part of your role as a school leader. Among other reasons, it's important for sustainability. If the one person in your school who holds all the knowledge and experience decides to leave, the remaining staff will be left in disarray and scrambling to learn and perform the tasks the leader carried out. Sustainability is emphasized in Jessica's work with helping schools in her district achieve STEM designation in Tennessee. Part of the process is developing a STEM action and sustainability plan for maintaining the work beyond the application year, acknowledging the need for a leadership team whose various stakeholders share ownership of the concept of a STEM school. With shared leadership, principals can leverage the collective wisdom and skills of the team to move the school toward its goals of earning—and sustaining—STEM designation.

It's crucial to recognize that staff serving in formal leadership roles within the school (e.g., instructional coaches, assistant principals, academic deans, deans of students) often have aspirations beyond their current positions. Creating a supportive environment means recognizing and addressing these aspirations. For instance, an instructional coach with a passion for technology integration might be given opportunities to lead workshops or spearhead initiatives related to STEM or educational technology.

Additionally, it's essential to avoid pigeonholing individuals into static roles. Providing opportunities for educational leaders to explore different facets of the field can broaden their perspectives through interactions with educators from other schools, districts, or even states. Opportunities for continued growth and learning can empower them to bring fresh ideas back to your school community. Ultimately, schools can cultivate a dynamic and forward-thinking educational environment by aligning leadership roles with personal passions and facilitating goal setting. Doing so not only benefits the individuals involved but also has a ripple effect on the entire school community, fostering a culture of continuous improvement and shared success.

> **Try This: Rotating Leadership**
>
> Rotate department or grade-level chairpersons so that everyone has the opportunity to develop leadership skills. It's not enough to just assign a title. Building capacity to serve as a chairperson requires mentoring from school leadership. If meetings are worth having, then preparation is worth doing. Meet with chairpersons before department or grade-level meetings to model how to plan for the meeting. Co-create an agenda with action items, clear outcomes, and structures for the engagement of participants. Remember to create *with* teachers (building capacity), not *for* them (building dependency). Provide time for chairpersons to ask clarifying questions, rehearse engagement strategies, and offer suggestions for improvement. Schedule time to reflect with chairpersons individually after their meetings to identify areas of success and growth.
>
> Another reason to rotate leadership roles is equity of compensation. Some leadership roles include a stipend. If one person continuously fills the position, others may come to resent the lack of opportunities for not only leadership growth but also financial gain.
>
> Serving in a leadership role broadens one's perspective and builds empathy. It's easier to be a reluctant participant when you never serve as the leader. An ideal outcome of rotating leadership is that the next time someone is not leading a meeting, they'll be more willing to participate.

## Leading Outside the School

Sometimes educators need to engage in experiences beyond their classroom, school, or district to grow. Professional organizations for content areas, educational roles, or specific topics provide some opportunities for leadership development. Many professional education associations and organizations offer teacher-leadership fellowships and access to resources, research, and connections, thus expanding members' knowledge base. Teachers can also lead within professional organizations by being active participants. Your school may have discretionary funding that can be used to pay for membership in these organizations. Funding teachers' attendance at a state or national conference can provide an additional layer of learning and networking. Leaders can even encourage teachers to propose conference presentations to share their knowledge and expertise with a broader audience. Even if their proposals are not selected, they can share information and resources with their school colleagues to build their capacity to design and deliver professional learning for peers. Leaders can set an expectation for department chairs to include relevant research and resources in discussions at department meetings or with individual department members.

Publishing is another avenue for cultivating leadership qualities. Teachers can write books or articles for educational journals. If such an undertaking seems overwhelming, suggest that teachers share their voices through podcasts or blogs.

Classroom teachers' unique perspective and firsthand experience makes them invaluable advocates for change in educational policy. There are many ways to engage in advocacy efforts and build capacity to influence policy. Locally, they can attend school board meetings to stay informed about local education policies, budget decisions, and curriculum changes. They can also use public comment periods to voice their concerns or suggestions. Teachers can actively participate in PTAs to collaborate with parents and community members on issues related to education. They can share insights into classroom needs and contribute to discussions on school improvement. Teachers can engage with local community organizations and leaders to build support for education initiatives and advocate for resources that benefit their students and schools.

Many states have teacher associations or unions that advocate for teachers' rights and quality education. Some organizations, such as Tennessee's State Collaborative on Reforming Education, advocate for student-focused policies. Joining these organizations provides teachers with a platform to collectively influence state education policy. Attending state-level conferences and workshops related to education policy and reform can help teachers stay informed about current issues and strategies for advocacy. Teachers can establish relationships with their state legislators, sharing their classroom experiences and insights on how policies affect students. They can also participate in advocacy days at state capitals.

Teachers can become active members of national teacher associations, which advocate for teachers and public education nationwide. Expanding on the publishing opportunities mentioned earlier, they can write op-eds or blogs to share their perspectives on education policy issues, which can have a national impact when published in reputable outlets. They can use social media platforms to connect with educators across the country and amplify their advocacy efforts on a national scale.

By collaborating with other educators both locally and nationally and joining or forming teacher-led advocacy groups or networks, teachers can contribute to a collective voice for education advocacy. Teachers should not underestimate the power of sharing their classroom experiences and success stories with policymakers, community members, and the public. Real-life examples and stories can illustrate the impact of policies on students and teachers.

In Tennessee, for example, TN Code §49-1-232 (2023) marks a significant stride in advancing computer science education in the state. This law, designed to bridge the digital divide, ensures that all public elementary, middle, and high school students have equitable access to comprehensive computer science coursework and resources. In addition to prioritizing student learning, the legislation recognizes the pivotal role of educators in this transformative journey. Teachers played a vital role in advocating for the law, sharing their firsthand experiences and insights into the impact of computer science education on student development. Through collaborative efforts, teachers not only influenced the creation of this policy but also secured provisions for a no-cost route for educators to earn an additional computer science endorsement. This comprehensive approach underscores the commitment to empowering students and educators alike in the realm of computer science education.

Teachers can engage in educational research and data analysis to provide evidence-based arguments in favor of certain policies or reforms. Some teachers decide to take their advocacy to the next level by running for local or state political office, where they can directly shape education policy.

By actively participating in advocacy efforts at the local, state, and national levels, teachers can leverage their expertise and experiences to support policies that promote better educational outcomes for their students and the broader community. Their voices are essential in shaping education policies that are practical, effective, and student-centered.

> **Try This: Role-Related Goals and Externships**
>
> Use annual summative evaluations and scheduled one-on-one conferences to help teachers develop their own professional goals, including goals that may mean a change of position or role. Identify the educator's strengths and be intentional about setting goals that help create and clear a path forward to their next role in education.
>
> At the same time, be sure the educator has a realistic notion of what a particular role involves. Often, the idea of a job is more appealing than the reality. When teachers express an interest or show aptitude for a particular role, schedule an externship for the teacher to shadow someone in that role. Getting a behind-the-scenes view will provide additional information and insight into the depth and breadth of the demands of the job. Follow up by asking the teacher reflection questions to help them process the experience. Debrief the externship and develop the next steps with the teacher.

## From Leaders to Ambassadors

As teachers ascend to leadership roles and eventually move on from your school, they won't completely leave their position behind. Instead, they will become ambassadors who carry your school's spirit and values wherever they go. Ideally, their experiences and growth within your school community has transformed them into advocates for quality education, effective leadership, and positive change. Just as they once inspired and guided students within your school walls, they will now inspire others with the wisdom and insights they gained from you.

These teacher leaders serve as living testaments to your school, forging lasting connections that extend far beyond your physical campus, and they're valuable because they can help attract high-quality candidates to your school. Investment in these highfliers yields tremendous benefits for the culture within your school and its reputation in the community.

## Empathy Episode

Read the following Empathy Episode and imagine what it would feel like to be in the teacher's position. Then use the reflection questions to consider leadership blind spots and how to remedy them.

You are a passionate and dedicated teacher who always dreamed of making a positive impact on students' lives and creating an engaging classroom learning environment. Despite your positivity, enthusiasm, and dedication, your principal seems disengaged and distant. He rarely takes the time to meet with you individually or the teachers as a group, leaving you feeling unheard and unsupported. You're always the first to volunteer for committees, organize school events, and take on extra administrative tasks. You long for opportunities to grow as a teacher leader, and you express this desire to your principal. He assigns you numerous extracurricular duties and responsibilities. Although you appreciate being involved and contributing to the school community, you wonder if your dedication is being taken for granted. You're never nominated for any professional growth programs, but you watch as other teachers are selected for specialized training, conferences, and leadership opportunities while you remain on the sidelines, your potential unrecognized.

You begin to feel stagnant and unsure of your own abilities. The lack of professional growth opportunities makes you question if you should stay at this school, despite the positive impact you believe you're making on the lives of your students. You question whether there's something you're doing that is causing the lack of investment and recognition from your principal. It isn't just about the missed professional learning opportunities and training programs; it's the feeling of being overlooked and undervalued that hurts the most.

## Reflection Questions

- How could the actions of the principal in the scenario be different if he chose to nurture the leadership potential of the teacher and build their capacity?
- What impact do the leader's actions have on the teacher and consequently on students?

The principal in this scenario is missing an opportunity to cultivate leadership potential within the teacher. If he were more engaged, he could recognize and appreciate the teacher's dedication. Regular individual or group meetings could provide a platform for the teacher to express her aspirations and for the principal to offer guidance and support.

School leadership includes the responsibilities of fostering growth and developing educators. If the principal in the scenario were more attuned to the teacher's ambitions, he could connect the teacher with relevant professional development opportunities, nominate the teacher for leadership programs, or at least acknowledge and praise her efforts. This kind of support would not only empower the teacher but also enhance the overall morale and effectiveness of the teaching staff.

The impact of the principal's actions on the teacher is clear—the teacher feels stagnant, undervalued, and unsure of her abilities. These feelings can lead to decreased motivation and job satisfaction, and possibly even a decision to leave the school. In turn, this lack of support and recognition could affect the students. A disheartened teacher may struggle to remain enthusiastic in the classroom, potentially affecting the quality of education and negatively influencing students. In addressing these blind spots, the principal can actively listen to the teacher's aspirations, provide meaningful opportunities for professional growth, and ensure that recognition is distributed fairly among the staff.

Building a culture of appreciation and support not only boosts individual morale but also contributes to a more positive and effective learning environment for everyone involved. Providing opportunities for teachers to lead both within and beyond the classroom fosters a sense of accomplishment, recognition, and professional growth. Each educator should set individual professional goals, and school leaders should work to connect educators with opportunities for professional growth. School leaders should ask questions to better understand the career aspirations of individual educators and provide opportunities for educators to develop the skills necessary to advance in their career.

## How Will You Commit?

- What strategies from this chapter are you committed to implementing?
- Who can help you implement these strategies?
- What outcome do you want to see as a result of implementing these strategies?

## Summary

In this chapter, we focused on the need for school leaders to nurture educators' leadership capacity both within and beyond the confines of the classroom and school. We delved into strategies for fostering a culture of continuous professional growth and the importance of professional development plans tailored to each teacher's strengths and aspirations. We also explored the broader impact of empowered educators who not only excel in their classrooms but actively contribute to the greater educational community, creating a ripple effect of positive influence.

# Conclusion: Your Next Steps in Inviting, Investing, and Inspiring

As you conclude this book, take a moment to reflect on the journey you've just embarked upon. The challenges facing education today are undeniable, but so too are the opportunities for growth, innovation, and profound impact. You've explored strategies to invite, invest in, and inspire educators—actions that are not just desirable but essential for building an irresistible school community.

Remember, the work of leadership is never truly done. Each day brings new possibilities to engage with your team, support their growth, and create an environment where both students and educators thrive. By embracing the practices outlined in this book, you're committing to a path of continuous improvement, one where your leadership makes a lasting difference.

Let go of the need for control and embrace the trust that empowers your educators to rise to their full potential. Trust that by fostering a culture of respect, belonging, and shared purpose, you will attract and retain the talented individuals who will shape the future of your school.

Your role as a leader is not just to manage but to inspire—to create a space where every member of your team feels valued and motivated to contribute their best. As you move forward, carry with you the lessons, insights, and strategies you've gained here. Apply them thoughtfully, adapt them as needed, and above all, remain committed to the well-being and success of your educators.

Thank you for your dedication to this critical work. The impact of your leadership will ripple outward, touching the lives of your students, your staff, and the broader community. As you continue to invite, invest in, and inspire your team, know that you are not just building a school—you are nurturing a vibrant, dynamic community that will flourish for years to come.

Happy leading, and may your journey be filled with purpose, passion, and the fulfillment that comes from being a catalyst for positive change.

# Appendix: Sample Peer Observation Tools

## Focus on Strategic Questioning

**Instructions:** Use this tool to observe and reflect on the use of **strategic questioning** during a lesson. Your goal is to identify specific examples of how the teacher's implementation of the practice supports student learning.

**What does strategic questioning...**

| Look like? | Sound like? |
|---|---|
| Describe specific actions you observe that demonstrate strategic questioning (e.g., the teacher moving around the room, using wait time). | Write down the actual questions you hear the teacher ask. Include both planned questions and spontaneous, in-the-moment questions. |
| The teacher paused after each question, giving students time to think. | "How does this concept connect with what we learned yesterday?" |
| The teacher circulated the room, engaging with different groups of students. | "Can you explain your reasoning for that answer?" |

**Reflection:**
- When *[teacher name]* asked *[strategic question]*, *[describe benefits for student learning]*.
- When *[teacher name]* *[took specific action]*, *[describe benefits for student learning]*.

When Ms. Smith asked, "What other strategies could we use to solve this problem?" it encouraged students to think critically and explore multiple solutions.

**Success criteria (identify at least three qualities of successful implementation):**
- Questioning includes both planned and spontaneous questions.
- Questions are sequenced to deepen student understanding (e.g., probing, assessing, advancing questions).
- Questions align with the lesson's clear learning target/objective/goal and build toward mastery of the standard.
- Students are given opportunities to share their thinking, both in writing and verbally.

## Focus on Academic Discourse

**Instructions:** Use this tool to observe and reflect on the use of **academic discourse** during a lesson. Your goal is to identify specific examples of how the teacher's implementation of the practice supports student learning.

**What does academic discourse…**

| Look like? | Sound like? |
| --- | --- |
| Describe specific actions you observe that demonstrate academic discourse (e.g., students discussing with peers, using academic language, actively listening to each other). | Write down examples of student dialogue you hear during the lesson. Include both planned opportunities for discussion and spontaneous student interactions. |
| Students turned to their partners to discuss the problem, referencing their notes. | "I agree with you because the text says…" |
| Students used sentence stems provided by the teacher to structure their responses. | "What you said reminds me of…" |

**Reflection:**
- When *[student name(s)]* discussed *[topic/concept]*, *[describe benefits for student learning]*.
- When *[student name(s)]* *[took specific action]*, *[describe benefits for student learning]*.

When the students engaged in a debate about the character's motives, it encouraged them to think critically and defend their interpretations.

**Success criteria (identify at least three qualities of successful implementation):**
- Students actively engage in discussions, using academic language relevant to the content.
- Conversations are sequenced and build upon previous knowledge, deepening understanding.
- Discussions are aligned with the lesson's clear learning target/objective/goal and contribute to mastery of the standard.
- Students have opportunities to express their thinking verbally and respond to peers' ideas.

# References

Adams, K., & Riding, L. (2006). The four stages of learning. *The Learning Journey*.
Barnum, M. (2023, March 6). *Teacher turnover hits new highs across the U.S.* Chalkbeat. https://www.chalkbeat.org/2023/3/6/23624340/teacher-turnover-leaving-the-profession-quitting-higher-rate/
Blanchard, K., & Conley, R. (2022). *Simple truths of leadership: 52 ways to be a servant leader and build trust*. Berrett-Koehler.
Broadwell, M. M. (1969). Teaching for learning. *The Gospel Guardian, 20*(41), 1–3a. https://edbatista.typepad.com/files/teaching-for-learning-martin-broadwell-1969-conscious-competence-model.pdf
Chapman, G., & White, P. (2019). *The 5 languages of appreciation in the workplace: Empowering organizations by encouraging people*. Northfield.
Covey, S. R. (1989). *The seven habits of highly effective people: Restoring the character ethic*. Simon & Schuster.
Cuddy, A. (2015). *Presence: Bringing your boldest self to your biggest challenges*. Little, Brown.
Dixon, D., Griffin, A., & Teoh, M. (2019). *If you listen, we will stay: Why teachers of color leave and how to disrupt teacher turnover*. The Education Trust and Teach Plus. https://files.eric.ed.gov/fulltext/ED603193.pdf
The Enneagram Institute. (n.d.). *The nine Enneagram type descriptions*. https://www.enneagraminstitute.com/type-descriptions/
Feiler, A. R., & Powell, D. M. (2016). Behavioral expression of job interview anxiety. *Journal of Business and Psychology, 31*, 155–171. https://doi.org/10.1007/s10869-015-9403-z
Goldring, R., Taie, S., & Riddles, M. (2014). *Teacher attrition and mobility: Results from the 2012–13 teacher follow-up survey: First look* (NCES 2014-077). U.S. Department of Education, National Center for Education Statistics. https://nces.ed.gov/pubs2014/2014077.pdf
Goleman, D. (2006). *Social intelligence: The new science of human relationships*. Bantam Books.
Guyton, M. (2022). How you love someone [Song]. UMG Recordings.
Hall, K. (2019). *Stories that stick: How storytelling can captivate customers, influence audiences, and transform your business*. HarperCollins Leadership.

Irwin, V., Wang, K., Tezil, T., Zhang, J., Filbey, A., Jung, J., Bullock Mann, F., Dilig, R., & Parker, S. (2023). *Report on the condition of education 2023* (NCES 2023–144). U.S. Department of Education, National Center for Education Statistics. https://nces.ed.gov/pubs2023/2023144.pdf

Klotz, A. C., & Bolino, M. C. (2022, September 15). When quiet quitting is worse than the real thing. *Harvard Business Review*. https://hbr.org/2022/09/when-quiet-quitting-is-worse-than-the-real-thing

Kurtz, H. (2022, April 14). A profession in crisis: Findings from a national teacher survey. *Education Week*. https://www.edweek.org/research-center/reports/teaching-profession-in-crisis-national-teacher-survey

Lowney, D. (Director), Sudeikis, J. (Writer), Lawrence, B. (Writer), & Hunt, B. (Writer). (2021, October 8). Inverting the pyramid of success (Season 2, Episode 12) [TV series episode]. In B. Hunt, J. Ingold, J. Kelly, B. Lawrence, J. Sudeikis, & B. Wrubel (Executive Producers), *Ted Lasso*. Ruby's Tuna.

McCrindle. (n.d.). *The generations defined*. https://mccrindle.com.au/article/topic/demographics/the-generations-defined/#boomers-section

Myers & Briggs Foundation. (n.d.). *Our legacy*. https://www.myersbriggs.org/my-mbti-personality-type/mbti-basics/c-g-jungs-theory.htm

Participant. (2013, January 24). *A pep talk from Kid President to you*. YouTube. https://www.youtube.com/watch?v=l-gQLqv9f4o

Pierson, R. (2013, May). *Every kid needs a champion*. TED. https://www.ted.com/talks/rita_pierson_every_kid_needs_a_champion

Pilat, D., & Krastev, S. (n.d.). *Why do we perform better when someone has high expectations of us? The Pygmalion effect, explained*. The Decision Lab. https://thedecisionlab.com/biases/the-pygmalion-effect

Reed, P. (Director). (2006). *The break-up* [Motion picture]. Universal Pictures, Mosaic, & Wild West Picture Show Productions.

Romansky, L., Garrod, M., Brown, K., & Deo, K. (2021, May 27). How to measure inclusion in the workplace. *Harvard Business Review*. https://hbr.org/2021/05/how-to-measure-inclusion-in-the-workplace

Siegel, D. J., & Bryson, T. P. (2020). *The power of showing up: How parental presence shapes who our kids become and how their brains get wired*. Ballantine Books.

Sinek, S. (2019). *The infinite game*. Portfolio/Penguin.

Snyder, A. (2020, October 3). *Pay it forward: The mental health benefits of giving back*. 1AND1. https://www.1and1life.com/blog/pay-it-forward/

# Index

The letter *f* following a page locator denotes a figure.

active listening, 83–84, 87, 100
acts of service *(5 Languages)*, 97
Adobe Creative Types test, 107
alcoholic beverage policy at social events, 67
appreciation
    and burnout avoidance, 137, 143–144
    as investment, 95-98, 99–100
artificial intelligence (AI) tools, 16, 33
authors' methodology, 4–6

body language, 41, 86, 97, 120, 139, 156
boundaries
    respecting, 122
    in social media use, 18
branding, 15–16
building tours for new hires, 52–54
burnout
    prevention, 122, 129
    rekindling burned-out teachers, 137–138

celebrations
    school-level, 11, 132
    of staff accomplishment, 142
classroom considerations, 53–54
collaboration. *See* teamwork and collaboration
communication
    active listening, 83–84, 87, 100

communication—*(continued)*
    casual conversation, 79–80
    conversations as investment, 85
    and focus, 84
    nonverbal communication and body language, 41, 86, 97, 120, 139, 156
    during onboarding process, 51
    presence and awareness, importance of, 83–84
    SOS (Solutions or Sighs) method, 84
    verbal contrasted with nonverbal, 44–45
community participation by school leaders, 20
Conscious Competence Learning Model, 105–106, 109
conscious goal monitoring, 130–131
control, relinquishing, 115–116
conversation. *See also* communication
    casual, 79–80
    empathetic listening, 87
    as investment, 85
Cooking Up Learning, 133–134

democratic methods, 136
diversity. *See also* inclusivity 134-136
    embracing differences on a team, 111–112
    historically underrepresented staff, 92–95, 95*f*

diversity—(*continued*)
    matrix for team decision making, 134–136, 135*f*
"dress down days," 96
Dunbar, Paul Laurence, 120

educational policy: advocacy for change, 159–160
emotional awareness, 85–87
empathetic listening, 87
Empathy Episodes
    inspiration and passion for teaching, 144–147
    interview process, 45–47
    leadership capacity, cultivation at group level, 161–163
    school identity, 20–22
    teachers, prioritization of, 99–100
    teamwork and collaboration, 124–125
    welcoming and onboarding process, 73–74
Enneagram test, 107
expectations
    addressed during onboarding process, 51, 64, 67
    and employee development, 123, 152
    for interview process, 34, 38, 40
    Pygmalion effect and power of, 103–106
externships, 161

failure, positive aspects, 117–119
*The 5 Languages of Appreciation in the Workplace*, 95
Four Stages of Competence, 105–106, 109
Four *S*s of showing up, 81–83, 82*f*
futurecasting, 13–14

Gartner Inclusion Index, 94–95
generational acceptance, 69–71
    intergenerational interaction, 108–109
goal monitoring, 130–131
Go-Round Protocol, 145–146
gratitude and appreciation, 143–144

"How You Love Someone," 143

"I can" mask, 122
"I don't care" mask, 122–123
"I know" mask, 121–122
"I'm good" mask, 121
"I'm OK" mask, 120
inclusivity
    culture of, 68–71
    inclusion index survey, 94–95
    matrix for team decision making, 134–136, 135*f*
    promotion of, 93
individualized education plans (IEPs), 57
*The Infinite Game*, 129
innovation, encouragement of, 117–118, 138
inspiration and passion for teaching. *See also* teachers
    collaborative problem solving, 141
    Diversity/Inclusivity Matrix, 134–135, 135*f*
    innovation, encouragement of, 138
    input and influence, encouragement of, 134–136
    negativity, overcoming, 139–142
    passion and purpose, connecting, 131–134
    protecting passion, 142–144
    purpose and goals, 129–131
    rekindling burned-out teachers, 137–138
    self-assessment, 127
    staff recognition, 136–137
    workplace culture and climate, 127–128
instructional materials, 56–57
intergenerational interaction, 69–71, 108–109
interview process, 23–24, 33–45
    candidate preparation, 38–40
    conducting the interview, 40–41
    consequences, unintended, 43–45
    in-person vs. online, 33
    interview prompts, 36–37*f*
    post-interview tasks, 41–43
    promptness, importance of, 34
    question development, 35
    rapid interview prep, 38
    résumé review, 37
    sample follow-up email, 42*f*

interview process—*(continued)*
    sample interview invitation, 39*f*
    scoring plans, 37–38
    self-assessment, 25
    team member roles, 35
    team preparation, 34–38

job satisfaction of teachers, 87–89

keys, classroom, 53–54

languages of appreciation, 95–98
leadership. *See also* servant leadership
    in the classroom, 153–154
    emotional intelligence, 85–87
    gratitude and appreciation, 143–144
    inviting input, 143
    leadership ecosystems, 149–152
    leadership stories, 14–15
    leading by example, 143
    leading outside the school, 158–160
    leading within the school, 156–157
    mental presence and emotional awareness, 83–84
    peer observation, 155
    physical presence, power of, 77–81
    relationships, investing in, 144
    rotating leadership, 158
    satellite desks, 80
    school ambassadors, 161
    scope of control, 3
    self-assessment, 150
    time audits, 80–81
licensure/certification, alternative, 33
love, belonging, and esteem, 89–92

magnet schools, 9–10
mascots, 15
masks, unmasking, and honesty, 119–123
Maslow's hierarchy of needs, 100, 105, 146. *See also* self-actualization
meetings
    assigned seats, 108
    Go-Round Protocol, 145–146
mentorship, 94
    and competence models, 109
    mentoring meeting checklist, 61–62, 61*f*

mentorship—*(continued)*
    M-n-M (mentor-and-mentee) meetings, 62–65
    of new hires, 59–66
    for struggling teachers, 113–114
merchandise, and school branding, 16
Merrimack College Teacher Survey, 2
micromanagement, 116
M-n-M (mentor-and-mentee) meetings, 62–65
mood checks, 128
Motivation by Appreciation Inventory, 96
multiclassroom leaders (MCLs), 156–157
multigenerational interaction, 69–71, 108–109
multitasking, dangers of, 83–84
Myers-Briggs Type Indicator, 108

nameplates, 54–55
negativity, overcoming, 139–142
new hires. *See* welcoming and onboarding process

orientation. *See* welcoming and onboarding process

peer observation, 106–107, 155
    academic discourse reflection tool, 168–169
    strategic questioning reflection tool, 167–168
physical touch *(5 Languages)*, 98
Point Out Practice (POP) Postcard strategy, 110
police department ride-along programs, 50
positivity
    overcoming negativity, 139–142
    "toxic positivity," 139, 140
presentation, power of, 28–29
professional development, 158–159
    designing a development program, 116–117
professional learning communities (PLCs), 153–154
professional organizations, 158–160
propinquity, concept of, 79–80

publishing, 159
purpose, school, 10–11. *See also* school culture and identity
Pygmalion effect, 103–106

quality time *(5 Languages)*, 97
"quiet quitting," 129

recruitment fairs, 24–32
    advertising, 29–30
    representatives, 30
    school spirit, 30–31
    sight lines, 28
    STARS of GOLD strategy, 27–32, 27*f*
    table and decor, 28–29
recruitment opportunities
    informal, 32–33
    recruitment fairs, 24–32
relationships
    investing in, 92–93, 144
    mentor–mentee, 59, 60, 111
    proximity and shared experiences, 79–80
    and team-building activities, 93–94
    and trust, 100, 103
*Report on the Condition of Education 2023*, 2
résumé review, 37
ride-along programs, 50
risk-taking and failure, 117–119

schedules, building-level, 11
school committees, 153
school culture and identity, 8–12
    actions and traditions, 11
    branding, 15–16
    positive vs. negative aspects, 43–44
    self-assessment of school identity, 9
    social media/digital presence, 17–20
    success stories, 12–15
    workplace climate and culture, 127–128
school events as recruitment opportunities, 32–33
school logo, 15
school mission, 10–11
school motto, 15–16
school spirit, 30–31
school websites, 19–20
self-actualization, 105, 146–147, 153. *See also* Maslow's hierarchy of needs
servant leadership, 116, 150–151. *See also* leadership
sheriff's department ride-along programs, 50
showing up for school leaders, Four *S*s of, 81–83, 82*f*
*Simple Truths of Leadership*, 116
*Social Intelligence*, 85
socialization for new hires, 67–68
social media strategies, 17–19
SOS (Solutions or Sighs) method, 84
special-interest clubs, 132
staff recognition, 136–137
state associations/unions, 159
sticker dot voting, 136
*Stories That Stick*, 12
storytelling
    futurecasting, 13–14
    leadership stories, 14–15
    and school identity, 11–12
    staff success stories, 12–13
    storytelling on social media, 17
    testimonials from community, 13
strengths showcase, 72
support for teachers
    collegial support for teachers, 48
    layered support models, 59–61
    mentorship of new hires, 59–66

tangible gifts *(5 Languages)*, 98
teachers. *See also* inspiration and passion for teaching; support for teachers
    appreciation as investment, 95–98
    conversation as investment, 85
    diversity, planning for, 95*f*
    emotions, impact of, 85–87
    focus, 84
    for historically underrepresented staff, 92–95
    job satisfaction, 87–89
    layered support models, 59–61
    love, belonging and esteem, need for, 89–92
    mental presence and emotional awareness, 83–84

teachers—(*continued*)
   physical presence of school leaders, 77–81
   resignation, reasons for, 88
   self-assessment, *77*
   showing up for school leaders, 81–83, 82*f*
   strengths and potential: identification and development, 107–109
   teacher feedback, 3
   teacher retention, current statistics, 2–3
   turnover, staff, deterring, 98–99
Teach for America, 33
team-building activities, 93–94
teamwork and collaboration
   Conscious Competence Learning Model, 105–106, 109
   control, relinquishing, 115–116
   diversity, embracing, 111–112
   doubts concerning a team member, 112–115
   over professional lifespan, 110–111
   peer observations, 106–107
   Point Out Practice (POP) Postcard strategy, 110
   professional development, 116–117
   Pygmalion effect, 103–106
   risk-taking and failure, 117–119
   self-assessment, 104
   strengths: identification and development, 107–109
   unconscious to conscious competence, 109–110
   unmasking and honesty, 119–123
technology
   and devices for teacher use, 56
   on-demand onboarding, 57
*Ted Lasso* (television series), 149

Tennessee, legislation in, 160
Tennessee State Collaborative on Reforming Education, 159
testimonials, 13
time audits for school leaders, 80–81
toxic positivity, 139, 140
turnover, staff
   impact of, 126–127
   prevention of, 98–99
   statistics, 126

websites, school, 19–20
welcoming and onboarding process
   building tours, 52–53
   civilian ride-along programs, 50
   classroom considerations, 53–54
   communication and introductions, 51–52
   community tours, 50
   culture of inclusivity, 68–71
   impact of, 72–73
   instructional materials, 56–57
   integration for new hires, 71–72
   mentors and supportive colleagues, 59–66
   nameplates, 54–55
   on-demand onboarding, 57
   orientation sessions, 58
   scheduling the process, 65–66
   self-assessment, 49
   social gatherings, 50
   socialization for new hires, 67–68
   team culture for, 66–67
   technology and devices, 56
   welcome kit, 49
   "who's who" charts, 51–52, *52*
"We Wear the Mask," 120
words of affirmation (*5 Languages*), 96–97
writing and publishing, 159

# About the Authors

 **Carrie Bishop** currently serves as an instructional coach at a middle school in Chattanooga, Tennessee. Previously she served as an academic lead, supporting school leadership teams at 19 schools serving students in grades K–12, and as a school-based instructional coach. Carrie has held various teacher leadership roles including new teacher mentor, grade-level team leader, and department chair and has hosted over a dozen preservice teachers. Twice during her 20-year career she has been named districtwide Teacher of the Year, and she also received a teacher leadership award from the Public Education Foundation. Earning both her bachelor's and master's degrees from the University of Tennessee at Chattanooga, Carrie also completed coursework at Carson Newman University and added K–12 administrative licensure. Carrie's passion lies in serving students and empowering those who guide and shape them for a brighter future.

 **Jessica Holloway** is a district innovation coach focusing on creative and innovative practices that provide transformative learning experiences for students. She coaches teachers and leaders in STEM education, computer science, and project-based learning. In her nearly 20 years in education, she has served in various roles including middle school language arts teacher, school-based instructional coach, new teacher mentor, team and department chair, district committee member, and professional learning facilitator. She is a 2019 ASCD Emerging Leader and a 2024 Google for Education Certified Innovator. Jessica holds a post-master's certificate in school leadership from the University of Tennessee at Chattanooga and a master's degree in education, specializing in adolescent literacy and technology, from Walden University. She was recently recognized by *EdTech Digest* as the 2022 EdTech Leadership award winner for school leadership, as the Tennessee STEM Innovation Network's 2022 Excellence in STEM Leadership awardee, and as ChaTech's TechX 2023 Tech Educator of the Year. Jessica is a champion for building the competence and confidence of educators so they can flourish as leaders.

## Related Resources: Teacher Recruitment and Retention

At the time of publication, the following resources were available (ASCD stock numbers in parentheses):

*Building a Strong Foundation: How School Leaders Can Help New Teachers Succeed and Stay* by Michelle Hope (#124015)

*Illuminate the Way: The School Leader's Guide to Addressing and Preventing Teacher Burnout* by Chase Mielke (#123032)

*Leadership for Learning: How to Bring Out the Best in Every Teacher* (2nd Edition) by Carl Glickman and Rebecca West Burns (#121007)

*Make Teaching Sustainable: Six Shifts That Teachers Want and Students Need* by Paul Emerich France (#123011)

*Still Learning: Strengthening Professional and Organizational Capacity* by Allison Rodman (#121034)

*Stop Leading, Start Building: Turn Your School into a Success Story with the People and Resources You Already Have* by Robyn R. Jackson (#121025)

*Support and Retain Educators of Color: 6 Principles for Culturally Affirming Leadership* by Andrea Terrero Gabbadon (#123018)

*What Can I Take Off Your Plate? A Structural—and Sustainable—Approach to Countering Teacher Burnout* by Jill Handley and Lara Donnelly (#125002)

For up-to-date information about ASCD resources, go to www.ascd.org. You can search the complete archives of *Educational Leadership* at www.ascd.org/el. To contact us, send an email to member@ascd.org or call 1-800-933-2723 or 703-578-9600.

The ASCD Whole Child approach is an effort to transition from a focus on narrowly defined academic achievement to one that promotes the long-term development and success of all children. Through this approach, ASCD supports educators, families, community members, and policymakers as they move from a vision about educating the whole child to sustainable, collaborative actions.

*Make Your School Irresistible* relates to the **engaged** and **supported** tenets. *For more about the ASCD Whole Child approach, visit* **www.ascd.org/wholechild.**

Become an ASCD member today!
Go to www.ascd.org/joinascd
or call toll-free: 800-933-ASCD (2723)

# WHOLE CHILD
# TENETS

### 1. HEALTHY
Each student enters school **healthy** and learns about and practices a healthy lifestyle.

### 2. SAFE
Each student learns in an environment that is physically and emotionally **safe** for students and adults.

### 3. ENGAGED
Each student is actively **engaged** in learning and is connected to the school and broader community.

### 4. SUPPORTED
Each student has access to personalized learning and is **supported** by qualified, caring adults.

### 5. CHALLENGED
Each student is **challenged** academically and prepared for success in college or further study and for employment and participation in a global environment.

**DON'T MISS A SINGLE ISSUE OF ASCD'S AWARD-WINNING MAGAZINE.**

# ascd educational leadership

If you belong to a Professional Learning Community, you may be looking for a way to get your fellow educators' minds around a complex topic. Why not delve into a relevant theme issue of *Educational Leadership*, the journal written by educators for educators?

Subscribe now, or purchase back issues of ASCD's flagship publication at **www.ascd.org/el**. Discounts on bulk purchases are available.

To see more details about these and other popular issues of *Educational Leadership*, visit **www.ascd.org/el/all**.

2800 Shirlington Road
Suite 1001
Arlington, VA 22206 USA

www.ascd.org/learnmore

www.ingramcontent.com/pod-product-compliance
Lightning Source LLC
Chambersburg PA
CBHW070554010526
44118CB00012B/1311